Donated by
Prolepsis Group
to The Heartland Institute
2015

DIALOGUE ON
John
Dewey

DIALOGUE ON

John Dewey

James T. Farrell

James Gutmann

Alvin Johnson

Horace M. Kallen

Harry W. Laidler

Corliss Lamont

Ernest Nagel

John H. Randall, Jr.

Herbert W. Schneider

Harold Taylor

Milton Halsey Thomas

Edited by CORLISS LAMONT

With the assistance of MARY REDMER

HORIZON PRESS   NEW YORK   1959

Copyright © 1959 by Horizon Press, Inc.

Printed in the United States of America
by H. Wolff Book Manufacturing Co., New York

ALL RIGHTS RESERVED

Library of Congress Catalog Card No. 59-14697

The transcription of an informal evening of reminiscences and personal impressions of John Dewey (1859–1952). Those participating were Professors James Gutmann, Ernest Nagel, John H. Randall, Jr., Herbert W. Schneider and Mr. Milton Halsey Thomas of Columbia University; Professor Horace M. Kallen of the New School for Social Research and Dr. Alvin Johnson, Director Emeritus of the New School; Dr. Harry W. Laidler, Director Emeritus of the League for Industrial Democracy; Dr. Harold Taylor, President of Sarah Lawrence College; Mr. James T. Farrell, author; and Dr. Corliss Lamont of Columbia at whose New York home the discussion took place in December 1958, and who has edited the manuscript with the assistance of Mary Redmer.

DIALOGUE ON

John Dewey

LAMONT

In recognition of John Dewey's Centennial, some of us thought it would be a good idea to spend an evening conversing informally about Professor Dewey, recalling our memories of him and making some estimate of his contribution to American life and perhaps the world at large. I think myself that John Dewey is the greatest philosopher that this country has yet produced; but that does not mean that he is way up on a pedestal and above criticism. So tonight I hope we may have a free, uninhibited flow of reminiscences, impressions and criticisms.

Mrs. Agnes Meyer had intended to come up from Washington for our discussion, but at the last minute found it was impossible. However, she did write a very nice letter, and I just want to quote a couple of lines from it in which she says: "I have known most of the distinguished people in politics, arts, and science for many a long year. Some of them, indeed, are my most intimate friends. But Dewey is the only one of whom I was continuously in awe as a thinker and a personality."

Well, we're very sorry Mrs. Meyer couldn't get here; and now, just to start the ball rolling, I would like to call on our John Dewey Professor at Columbia, Ernest Nagel.

NAGEL

I take it that this is an occasion on which all of us, if we so desired, could spend our time manifesting our piety toward Dewey, piety in the sense in which Santayana characterized it as "an attachment to the sources of one's being." We could all exercise this virtue without pretense, since each of us here can rightfully acknowledge John Dewey as the source of at least a part of his intellectual being. However, I share Corliss Lamont's attitude that we are not gathered here to hold a memorial meeting, with the intent to express our indebtedness to Dewey and to voice our praises of him. At any rate, I hope that we will take our admiration of Dewey pretty much for granted, and that we will spend the evening in recalling our personal experiences with him so as to reveal aspects of his qualities with which some of us have perhaps had no direct acquaintance. I myself did not enjoy the privilege of knowing Dewey intimately; and I am therefore extremely eager to hear the reminiscences of those who did.

A few moments ago Dr. Johnson mentioned Dewey's ability to mix a strong drink. Let me contribute a bit of evidence in support of Dr. Johnson's remark. I remember one memorable occasion when the late Otto Neurath sought to interest Dewey in the Unity of Science movement, by having him contribute a monograph to the *Encyclopedia of Unified Science* which Neurath was then planning. I accompanied Neurath and Sidney Hook when they called on Dewey at his home; and Neurath was having obvious difficulty in obtaining Dewey's participation in the *Encyclopedia* venture. Dewey had one objection—there may have been others, but this is the only one I recall—to Neurath's invitation. The objection was that since the Logical Positivists subscribed to the belief in atomic facts or atomic propositions, and since Dewey did not think there are such things, he could not readily contribute to the *Encyclopedia*.

Now at that time Neurath spoke only broken English, and his attempts at explaining his version of Logical Positivism were not very successful. Those of us who knew Neurath will remember his elephantine sort of physique. When he realized that his efforts at explanation were getting him nowhere, he got up, raised his right hand as if he were taking an oath in a court of law (thereby almost filling Dewey's living room), and solemnly declared, "I *swear* we don't believe in atomic propositions." This pronouncement won the day for Neurath. Dewey agreed to write the monograph, and ended by saying, "Well, we ought to celebrate," and brought out the liquor and mixed a drink.

Neurath never drank, as a matter of principle. He was a prominent figure in the Social Democratic movement in Vienna; and like other leading figures in the movement, he wished to set an example to Viennese youth, and so abstained from all alcoholic beverages both in public and in private. But on this occasion he made an exception, and accepted the glass Dewey offered him. I concluded that Neurath must have had a good deal of experience with alcohol before he became a Social Democrat, for he stood the drink very well. I certainly did not, for I found it very potent.

FARRELL

I can add something here. Otto Neurath once came to my house and drank about a gallon of milk during an all-night talk. John liked Otto and considered him the one empiricist—or the one pragmatist—in the Logical Positivist movement. I recall that I took a course in symbolic logic at NYU in 1941, and John advised me not to. His reason for this was his opposition to the Logical Positivists. He considered them all scholastics, with the exception of Neurath. So out of the meeting he came to like Otto Neurath.

I want to make another remark. I just want to disagree with Ernest Nagel on the question of piety. I don't think it is piety to remember with warmth a man who was not only a great man but a man one loved.

KALLEN

How about piously loving God?

FARRELL

No. I never looked at John as God. I looked at him as a good friend and a great man.

RANDALL

I don't think he ever evoked awe in people.

FARRELL

No, he didn't, but he did inspire love.

KALLEN

He seemed to me to have evoked awe.

LAMONT

Well now, Herbert Schneider was Dewey's assistant here in the early days when he came to Columbia, isn't that right?

SCHNEIDER

Not *that* early! * I'm not *that* old. [*Laughter.*]

* Dewey started teaching at Columbia in 1904 as Professor of Philosophy.

But it was—oh, in 1917, I guess. However, I'd like to start with Dewey's early days, which were much earlier than mine. We tried to get him to reminisce. And it was very difficult. I think on principle Dewey wouldn't reminisce. He liked to look forward to the future, and he certainly liked to keep *au courant* with the present. But to get him to reminisce about his early days was very difficult. Finally, at some birthday dinner we gave for him we bought him a copy of Marsh's edition of Coleridge's *Aids to Reflection* and asked him whether this recalled anything to his mind. Then he opened up, and said, "Yes, I remember very well that this was our spiritual emancipation in Vermont. Coleridge's idea of the spirit came to us as a real relief, because we could be both liberal and pious; and this *Aids to Reflection* book, especially Marsh's edition, was my first Bible."

KALLEN
Herbert, do you remember him saying "pious, both liberal and pious"? Did he say "pious"?

SCHNEIDER
Yes, I think so. Anyway, I wouldn't swear to

that, but I think so. And then we said, "Well, when did you get over Coleridge?" He said, "I never did. Coleridge represents pretty much my religious views still, but I quit talking about them because nobody else is interested in them." Well, I thought that was a rather interesting comment on his tactics as well as on his faith. That little bit of reminiscence we got out of him, but he would say very little more about his career—at least I never heard him talk very much about it; perhaps some of the rest of you have. And all the years that I knew him in academic life his conversation was confined largely to current issues and what he called "the problems of men."

He was especially interesting in his preparation for his two ethics courses. He gave psychological ethics one year, and then moral and political philosophy the next year, and alternated. It was part of his general philosophy to do that—what he called theoretical ethics and practical ethics. And he would prepare the outline very carefully, and the references; and then he forgot about the outline. But the students were supposed to follow the outline, even though he didn't. And it made the course very interesting, because we had systematic reading and unsystematic doctrine.

KALLEN

Certainly a help—the doctrine. I have a friend in Chicago, Mr. I. B. Lipson, who's a very distinguished member of the Illinois bar. He was a pupil of Dewey's at Ann Arbor—at the University of Michigan; and I asked him what he could remember, and he wrote me a couple of pages of notes which I'd like to read to you.

LAMONT

Please do.

KALLEN

These are immediate and personal:

"I was in his seminar in ethics the spring semester of 1894; I'm probably the last survivor of that class. [He's 86 now.] It was from 4 to 6 p.m.; usually one or another of the children would come in, open the door and shout, 'John, are you ready to go home?' He nearly always managed to get rid of the kid or else bring him up on the platform where the child remained a competitor for the attention of the class. It was a warm spring, a small class, and some of them were disrespectful enough to snooze a little during the discussion, but Dewey didn't mind. I remember writing a thesis for that class entitled 'Motive and Intention.' I must have seen some deep philosophical distinction and at that time it must have seemed very important to me.

"I think Dewey went to Chicago the following autumn. By the way, during that year I roomed in the house adjoining his. I think he possessed the noisiest typewriter in the world and it seemed always to be clattering at the wrong time.

"Did I ever tell you that the first time I met him was at football practice, standing next to him out on the campus? From what I said he probably guessed I was a freshman, and he was telling me about the players and the game. That was before there was an athletic field in Ann Arbor or perhaps anywhere else. Practice was right on the campus and there was always a crowd. At the close he and I walked in the same direction. As we were about to separate I gave him my name and said I hoped to see him again. It took a lot of courage to say that because he wore a weak little mustache and I took it for granted he was an upperclassman. He said he hoped he would see me too; he said, 'My name is John Dewey.' I did a double take on that, but managed to say, 'You mean Professor Dewey?' He said yes in a rather offhand way. I was too scared to say anything more. He must have been 31 or 32 years of age at that time and looked much younger.

"The following year I took psychology under Lloyd who subsequently became the head of the department. Our textbook was the one written by Dewey—all I remember of it was this: that perception is the apperception of the apperceptive processes. I never believed it and I don't now. By the way, I remember his telling us once to take some courses under George Herbert Mead * who had been a student under Münsterberg. Mead called the course physiological psychology. Dewey told us that all 'introspective psychology' had come to an end; the new psychology was what Mead was teaching. I took a course under Mead. All I remember of it was that we dissected frogs in the basement of the

---

* Professor Mead taught philosophy at the University of Michigan, 1891–1894; and at the University of Chicago, 1894–1931.

old Lit. building. I had just turned 17—five days younger than my grandson John was just one week ago—figure that one out."

LAMONT

Jim Farrell, you were going to say something—

FARRELL

I was going to say, I had the same impression. In Mexico City in 1937 I wanted to talk to him about William James and particularly about George Herbert Mead, whose work I've always been enthusiastic about. He didn't indulge much in personal reminiscence. Of course he had a great respect for James and a warm and abiding feeling of friendship for Mead. John couldn't really appear on a platform with Hutchins because of the fight at the University of Chicago in 1931 when Mead and some of the other members of the Department of Philosophy resigned. But, to repeat, he didn't indulge in personal reminiscence.

KALLEN

You mean about Mead?

FARRELL

Yes. But it was the same with many people; for instance, I asked him about Randolph Bourne, and he didn't reminisce much. He'd speak about a man's ideas or what he thought of him. He also had a great deal of wisdom. Many people came to him with problems, and he'd make very acute, direct, simple comments.

KALLEN

Certainly after he came East all the influences on him were not from books but also from people. It was certainly the case in Chicago, in relation to Jane Addams and Hull House.

FARRELL

An interesting trait of Dewey's was that he would always listen to young people; he was extremely attentive to any young person. He was a good listener. You generally won't find philosophers—I'm not talking about those in this room—men like Dewey, who *listen* as much as John would. Really, he'd listen, and listen, and listen. I even talked him to sleep one night.

TAYLOR

I'd like to pick that up, in terms of my own experience with John Dewey. I came to the East in 1945; Max Otto had written to John that I was coming and would John please be nice to me; and Max had asked me to call him and announce my arrival, which I did. The first conversation I recall was down at his apartment on Fifth Avenue in which immediately he began talking about a graduate student who had just written him a letter to which he had just replied. We were plunged into a discussion of what the graduate student had said and the degree of misunderstanding which was accumulating around his own philosophy. John made the point at some length that it was up to the young people to rediscover the things which he had written originally and not be fooled by commentators on things he had written, say ten years before or twenty years before.

I found significant Dewey's impulse to think of the young people coming on, to take seriously anything they said, and to *reply*, no matter how wild the person was who wrote to him and how silly it seemed. But this real concern that some important thing might be said by a young person, which he had the responsibility to reply to—that's the first impression I had of him. He was a very great person.

KALLEN

That was true also of James and Santayana. Both of them also replied to every question that almost anybody that I know of wanted to ask. And James often at great elaboration—just as Dewey—and Santayana, as you know.

LAIDLER

When I was at their home during Dewey's 90th Anniversary affair, Mrs. Dewey said, "Oh, John got a great kick this afternoon. He was on the Fifth Avenue bus when a man came up and said, 'Oh, you're John Dewey! I want to introduce you to my daughter.' And he introduced him to the daughter, ten or eleven years of age, who beamed at him and said, 'Oh, you're John Dewey! Why, we're using John Dewey's *Education* in our class.'" That, said Mrs. Dewey, gave John more satisfaction than some college professor's talking about following the John Dewey philosophy or Dewey educational system.

FARRELL

I want to come back to John's letters. There was

an amusing incident about an intellectual Catholic in Washington who wrote letters to me denouncing John; and then wrote letters to John telling him that I was a renegade. John and I exchanged the letters, and then finally Dewey wrote him a brief letter; in two or three of the most apt sentences he nailed the man for his lack of compassion and charity. It was very neat. But he did write all his own letters, many of them in longhand.

KALLEN
Did he ever talk to you or write to you about Matthias Alexander?

FARRELL
Not very much. He had said that at one time he had believed in—had been interested in him. But he never said much about him; that's all I recall.

SCHNEIDER
Dewey thought Alexander had done him a lot of good.

FARRELL
Yes. Oh, he said that. That's all he said.

KALLEN

He and James Harvey Robinson * introduced me to Alexander. I tried to persuade Ernest here at one time, when he was having the same trouble that I had, to see Alexander, but he scorned it. I said that Dewey had had relief, but he thought Dewey was superstitious.

JOHNSON

Well, Dewey was enamored of Alexander, so that when Alexander wrote a book and Randolph Bourne reviewed it pretty harshly, Dewey declared he'd write no more for *The New Republic* if we allowed Randolph Bourne to write for us. It was a terrible blow to Randolph, who was a great admirer of Dewey.

LAMONT

Well, now, about Alexander, was he concerned with your posture and that sort of thing?

GUTMANN

Yes. *Man's Supreme Inheritance* was the name of the book, and Dewey wrote the introduction to it.

* Professor of History at Columbia, 1892–1919.

Dialogue on Dewey

KALLEN

Dewey wrote introductions not only to *Man's Supreme Inheritance,* which he got me to review for *The Dial,* but also to two other books of Alexander's. Alexander I met through Robinson and Dewey; we had got to talking about the whole problem of bodily stance, and movement—the Delsarte teaching and so on. I don't remember what the occasion was, but I know that Delsartism came into the conversation somehow.

This was when I was teaching at Columbia's summer session. It must have been 1917, because we used to go, a gang of us, to a movie and stand up when they played "The Star Spangled Banner" and the "Marseillaise," regularly.

GUTMANN

Your class was in the same room as Dewey's and an hour before, as I recall. Is that correct?

KALLEN

Yes. They took me down to Alexander, who was living at the Hotel Leonori with his brother; and Alexander asked me to dinner. We had dinner in his workshop with his brother, and he served champagne—which was an extraordinary and interesting episode. And then he told me that he'd been preparing a new book and wanted to know if I would review it. Well, I couldn't be committed unless somebody would ask me to; and Dewey saw to it that I was asked.

Dewey told me that at one time he suffered from a very stiff neck, and that he had had difficulty with his eyes. I think it was through Robinson (James Harvey) that he came to Alexander; and he said that Alexander had completely cured him, that he was able to read and to see and move his neck freely. Now Alexander's technique was a rather dubious one; it had been developed and elaborated in a variety of ways. Alexander told me that he had gotten his idea by reading James. And then he seemed to have forgotten about James and used the formula "ideomotor attitude"—no, not *attitude*, but some other term that went with *ideomotor* which he had gotten from James's *Psychology*. And in his own formulation what he called "the position of mechanical advantage" was a central idea. He said that every body was askew, every body had developed bad postural habits, that posture irradiated a body's feelings and thinking, that therefore, if you could establish correct posture, you could correct everything posture involves. It was not only a universal constant, but a scheme of universal salvation.

Dewey didn't take to the salvation, but he did get something out of the physiology, as applied later, say, in Mabel Todd's *The Thinking Body*, and implied in Walter Cannon's *The Wisdom of the Body*. Alexander held there's a natural way of sitting, standing, running, walking and so on—a correct unlearned condition of the muscles. But the ways of the society we grow up in make us crooked and sick. To be straightened out, we must take thought and learn how to recover the naturally right posture. To show me, Alexander put me in a chair, placed a carpet-covered brick at my back, and altered my posture with his hands. Then he had me stand up and walk, and sit, walk, sit, move around, again and again. I took Judge Julian Mack down to him once, and Julian couldn't see the good of it at all. He went once but never again.

GUTMANN

Jack Randall and I were in a small group to whom Robinson sang the praises of Alexander, and told how Alexander had cured him of holding his head to one side. The only difficulty was that throughout the conversation Robinson sat there talking about it with his head on one side. So it wasn't quite convincing.

But I think, Mr. Johnson, if we're going to keep the record straight, you must have a detail inexact. If Bourne was devoted to Dewey and resented the suggestion that he no longer review for *The New Republic*, that must have been some years after he published in *The Seven Arts*, at the time of the outbreak of the First World War, an article on Dewey with the significant title, "Twilight of Idols." So I think something must be a little different in that particular record.

KALLEN

Man's Supreme Inheritance must have appeared in '18 or early '19.

GUTMANN

Yes. And the *Seven Arts* article was 1917 at the latest.

KALLEN

Incidentally, the American edition was the second edition. There had been an earlier edition in England, I think in 1910 or '12.

FARRELL

Years later, I pressed Dewey on all these questions. I was too brash. I recall that on the train going to Mexico in 1937 I pressed him very hard on Randolph Bourne. John showed no animus, and he said in his calm way that Bourne was extremely clever and gifted, but he did not have depth. It was evident that John was speaking without animus.

KALLEN

He had curious reticences. There was this man, Franklin Ford—in Michigan—to whom he was intellectually indebted; and I once raised a question about him; and all that John would say was, "He turned out to be a scoundrel." But this had no bearing on the original interpretation of Ford's views about the development of industrial civilization and so on. Dewey had a long reference to Ford in a letter to James, as I recall.

NAGEL

There was another man with whom Dewey had

some intellectual relations which broke up in hurt feelings on one side. Do you remember a man named Klyce? Did you know him?

KALLEN

Yes, Scudder Klyce, a healer. I didn't know him personally, but I knew three of his patients.

NAGEL

Dewey makes acknowledgments in one of his books to some of Klyce's views. Klyce wrote a book called *The Universe*. Morris Cohen once told me that Klyce had submitted the manuscript to Harcourt, who asked Cohen to report on it. Cohen recommended it for publication, but with the qualification that while the book had many interesting things in it, "it was twice as long as it need be." Harcourt then informed Klyce that they would publish the book provided he cut it in half. But Klyce was angered, and would have none of this. However, he apparently could find no other publisher. He therefore bought a printing press, and started to set up the type. But he found the job so long and laborious that he finally shortened his manuscript by half, and printed only the briefer version. [*Laughter.*]

Klyce subsequently maintained that Dewey had promised to collaborate with him in writing a book on logic. It's obvious, however, that Dewey had had no such intentions. When Dewey's *Logic* finally appeared, Klyce was infuriated, and published a book of his own called *Dewey's Suppressed Psychology*.

KALLEN
Yes, I remember it. I remember the title. I didn't read it.

LAMONT
Herbert, going back to your assistantship, what was it like, being assistant to John Dewey?

SCHNEIDER
Well, I was just reminiscing a little while you were talking about his listening to graduate students. And I remember the first essay I had to write for Dewey—it was, I think, on Rousseau—and I turned it in to him, and he began reading it right away. He just had me sit there a little, and then he looked out the window a little. He said, "Well, I hadn't thought about this this way. You have something there. You better work on that." And I felt

flattered of course. Then later on, when I was sharing the office with him, I realized that he said that to all the graduate students. [*Laughter.*] It was very effective. It wasn't merely tactics, though. It was genuine generosity.

FARRELL

There was nothing false about his generosity. I remember I asked him why he wrote so many introductions. There was particularly one book I didn't think was worthy of an introduction by him. He said, well, in this case the writer showed some promise, and if he wrote an introduction it would not only help the book but it would also stimulate a young philosopher to do better.

TAYLOR

I had the feeling that—whether it was a deliberate refusal to be discriminating about graduate students or the young people he was encouraging, it appeared to me that no matter who said what, he encouraged the student. I was a little bewildered when I was asked to sit and listen to letters or asked to read papers that people had sent to him. Some of the damnedest things that I wouldn't spend the time on, but he would read them all and write back. He seemed to pay no attention to whether they were bad or good. There were some very dreary things written by education students about him and his views, which I didn't think a man of his quality should waste his time on. John would tire himself out responding and reading and thinking about what had been sent, and say, "Well, this fellow has something." John made an honest effort to help everybody.

RANDALL
He suffered fools gladly.

FARRELL
A point has to be made clear here. He had firmness of character. He knew how to say no. I know several times I tried like hell to get him to do things; he'd say, "No!" And he meant it. If he didn't believe in something, he'd say, "No," unmistakably; and you couldn't move him.

SCHNEIDER
He'd also say some rather sharp things in a very un-sharp way. I remember one evening we were

coming home in the subway from listening to Bertrand Russell expound the way in which public utilities should be put into public hands. It was a crowded car, and I can still see him scratching his head as he held onto the strap. He turned to me, and he said, "Come to think of it, I have never seen any hands that weren't private. Have you?"

FARRELL

I recall that once in Key West he was writing a reply to Russell for *The Journal of Philosophy*, and he made the strongest statement I ever heard him make on Russell. He said, "You know, he gets me sore." [*Laughter.*] I think Russell was unfair in his criticism of Dewey's ideas.

KALLEN

Russell would rather make a wisecrack than a correct observation.

LAMONT

Did Dewey ever know Russell personally?

FARRELL

He knew Russell in China.

KALLEN

Oh, that Dewey-Russell-China story!

LAMONT

What happened in China?

KALLEN

Well, Bertie was over there with Dora, and Mrs. Dewey (*not* Roberta *) was not keen on seeing them. Then Russell got pneumonia, and there was a great to-do among the Chinese. They were hoping he would die because it was so long since a sage had died in China. [*Laughter.*] And at that time one of my former pupils at the New School, who was a YWCA secretary in Peking, wrote that the YWCA was taking care of Dora, and that at last Mrs. Dewey allowed some kind of intervention and some help and contact with the Russells in China. Now that may be apocryphal, but I'm inclined to believe that it's correct.

FARRELL

You know, Dewey was the one who arranged for Russell to have a job at the Barnes Foundation in

* The second Mrs. John Dewey.

Philadelphia. I don't know what happened or why; but Dewey arranged it because Russell was looking for some kind of a post.

KALLEN

Well, between Barnes and Russell, Dewey would naturally have had a very difficult diplomatic problem.

FARRELL

I would guess so. There's one other point you made. I recall that during the period of celebrations of his 90th birthday there was an affair at Columbia for him at which President Eisenhower was chairman. Afterwards I went home with John and Roberta, and he started bringing out books and talking: Had I read this book? Was this fellow a fellow traveler? Did I hear about this book? And he started taking off his shirt; he was tired; his mind was good, but he was frail. And then he finally said, "Ah, I've got to go to bed." He wanted to keep talking about new books; he had an insatiable curiosity; he lived constantly in his time—that's the feeling I had about him—that he lived in the present.

NAGEL

Jim, talking about this, I remember on this one occasion when I went to see Dewey with Neurath—I think while we were getting our coats in the hall—he had a great number of books on the table; and there was one by Hocking. One of us asked Dewey whether he had seen this. He said, no, he hadn't got around to it. We turned the pages, and this book was dedicated to Dewey; but he hadn't opened it to the extent of finding it was dedicated to him.

FARRELL

Well, I know of many instances in which the opposite was true, and every once in a while he'd drop me a note and suggest a book for me to read. I must say this in talking about Dewey; Dewey always said this, "Jim Farrell's a good literary critic and writer; he's no philosopher." [*Laughter*.] He would have dismissed anything I said on philosophy.

KALLEN

That's what Royce suggested about Dewey. I remember the first time I ever saw Dewey was at a meeting of the American Philosophical Association which was held in Cambridge—it might have been the first meeting. Dewey was expounding some pragmatic point; and Royce got up to cross-question him (I was still a student) and seemed to endeavor to trap him in contradiction. The questioning had something to do with the nature of identity; and I remember the striking way in which Dewey indicated that when you say, "I is I," or "A is A," one A is active. Identity is a process of identification, and not just an antithesis of two A's.

I see that very slim, black mustachioed, black-haired figure, still talking with the kind of slow cadence, the hesitant rhythm that characterized Dewey's communication. As Ernest used to say, you could see him think. And I see Royce with his high-pitched, almost juvenile voice sharply presenting questions, and this almost feline inattention to the intention of the speaker in Dewey's follow-through of his own thought.

FARRELL

I think that he would constantly think through the same problem when he talked. This was even more the case with Mead. Dewey and Mead did not want their ideas to become over-crystallized; they didn't want to commit themselves to a formulation to the degree that they couldn't revise it.

SCHNEIDER

There's one problem that I never could solve, though. In this meditative cadence that he had, he almost always would come out with a heavy accent on the prepositions; and I never could figure out why. But almost invariably—

KALLEN

It might have been a residue from too much Hegelian reading.

LAMONT

In his courses—at Columbia, for instance—was he ever what you would call a popular teacher or lecturer with the students?

SCHNEIDER

His classes were well attended; but the lectures weren't well listened to, so that he was popular in one sense, but not as a lecturer. But the notes! If we stayed awake enough to take notes, the notes that we got were wonderful to read.

NAGEL
Yes, you had to take notes to keep awake.

GUTMANN
What you said at the beginning, though, about the preparation that was then disregarded—there was a syllabus, but he could easily depart from it —ties in with what Farrell said just a moment ago. I think there was no other teacher I ever had who gave such a sense that for fifty minutes you were watching a man think; and the symbolic conclusion always for me was—I don't know whether the rest of you remember it—that he would take the notes which he'd brought along (I don't know how extensive they were), often on yellow paper, and crunch them up as though to say, "I've thought it through, now I've said it, and next time I'll think again and throw that paper down on the desk or on the floor." I remember saying to Irwin Edman once that this was to me the symbol of the way Dewey constantly was working at his ideas; and Irwin characteristically said, Yes, if anyone had ever bothered to pick up those papers, there would have been the makings of quite a dissertation in them.

SCHNEIDER

But most of them Dewey must have picked up because when I got his desk, his desk was full of those crumpled papers. [*Laughter.*]

KALLEN

Were those notes typewritten? Were they typed?

GUTMANN

Yes.

KALLEN

Do you know when he first took to a typewriter?

VOICE

Probably in Chicago.

GUTMANN

Well, no, you have your letter there; he had a typewriter at Ann Arbor.

KALLEN

He'd been using it at Ann Arbor in 1894, and that must have been about the time of the birth of the typewriter.

THOMAS

That goes back to about 1876. I just want to add, I took a course with him once, and I don't recall that he ever looked at the class during the whole course. He always seemed to be talking to someone up in Kent Hall. [*Laughter.*] And I had the feeling of actually watching thought going on; it seemed quite laborious. I mean, he was so honest, he had to define everything, he had to think around it, and when he had finished his excursion, he would resume the main thread of his remarks in the next sentence without warning. It was not only confusing, but placed a heavy strain on orderly note-taking.

KALLEN

It seemed to me that he was much more at ease in communication with his typewriter than he was face to face, person to person. There was a kind of withdrawn quality in all his communication, I found. Even at moments of strong feeling there seemed, not reserve, not a holding back, but yet some sort of barrier. You came across to him, but he didn't come across to you.

FARRELL

John was shy.

KALLEN
I'm sorry?

FARRELL
He was a shy man.

KALLEN
Well, the sadness has been variously attributed to the death of his young child, a boy, and then a second son died. There have been other attributions, but I don't know that he was intrinsically sad. Maybe he was—

FARRELL
No, I didn't say *sad,* I said *shy.* Shy.

KALLEN
Shy? There may be something related—between shyness and sadness.

TAYLOR
I have one memory to contribute that remains vivid with me. Along about 1947, I believe it was, John thought it would be great if Albert Barnes's Collection came into our hands at Sarah Lawrence

College. He wrote to Albert Barnes and said he had a college president in tow and wanted us to come to know each other with a view to having the Barnes Collection made a part of the art program at Sarah Lawrence because, he said, "The art program at Sarah Lawrence is so much in line with my own thinking and with the kind of thinking which you're doing, Albert, that you should meet this fellow and see if you can't do business."

We arranged to go to the Barnes place one weekend. John was to go too. But he wasn't feeling well enough to go, and launched me solo with Albert Barnes. After taking about a day and a half of abuse by Barnes down at his place, I said, "I'm sorry I'm just not interested in coming back every Tuesday to listen to you lecture, because I can't take the time. I know about what you think, but I can't come to Philadelphia every Tuesday to join your class." There was a mutual agreement that it was time for us to leave for home. If I hadn't left, I think he'd have wanted to throw me out.

I talked with John about it, and for about six or eight weeks after that we did our best to find some way in which Albert Barnes and I could accommodate our views to each other. The relationship of

Barnes to Dewey I found interesting in that Dewey was the only person, I think, in the world, who could do anything with Barnes. The effort that John made to link up that art collection with Sarah Lawrence College was extraordinary; but he could not understand that the man himself was so difficult to everyone but John Dewey that it would be impossible for anyone but Barnes himself to take that Collection into immortality.

KALLEN

My guess is that the only thing that Dewey could do with Barnes was a function of what Barnes believed he could do with Dewey.

TAYLOR

I just wondered if anyone else had any stories or memories of the relationship with Barnes. It seems to me to be a fascinating one.

SCHNEIDER

For a whole semester Barnes attended Dewey's seminar—I think it was group ethics or something of the sort. He never said anything; he was just an attentive member of the class.

RANDALL

For one whole year Barnes came to Columbia for Dewey's one-o'clock class. It was right after lunch, and Barnes would promptly fall—he'd sit in the front row and then promptly fall asleep. [*Laughter.*] And when the bell rang and class went out, and Dewey would gather up his books, Barnes usually woke up, but a good deal of the time he didn't; and Dewey would turn around and smile at him and go out the door, leaving him sleeping there. [*Laughter.*]

KALLEN

The summer I was at Columbia a group, of whom Irwin Edman was one, were making a study under Dewey's leadership of certain ostensibly seditious groups in Philadelphia, and Barnes was footing the bill. They were going down—were you in that?

GUTMANN

No, it wasn't a matter of sedition; it was Polish nationalism, as I recall, and the—

KALLEN

Well, Barnes gave the impression that it was sedition.

GUTMANN

Oh, I don't know what Barnes said about it, but I'm quite sure it was primarily a study of nationalism. As to what Harold Taylor said about their relationship, Dewey really seems to have been the only one of Barnes's friends who didn't ultimately quarrel with Barnes.

LAMONT

Well, Barnes helped him with his book on aesthetics.* Dewey gives him thanks in his introduction there. That is, he learned a great deal from Barnes, didn't he?

VOICES

I'm not so sure. He used the Barnes Collection.

SCHNEIDER

Wasn't that book done, a good deal of it, on shipboard? Barnes had him on shipboard where he couldn't get away during the whole ocean voyage.

* *Art as Experience*, 1934.

TAYLOR

Is it true that Barnes was the chief instrument for getting John interested in and working on aesthetics?

SCHNEIDER

Painting, but not poetry. Dewey had a—

RANDALL

Dewey was always interested in poetry.

LAMONT

And actually wrote some himself.

SCHNEIDER

Poetry, yes; but I think that as far as painting goes Barnes's influence was very great.

FARRELL

He was interested in novels and literature. I know that around his 90th birthday he was recommending Joyce Cary.

SCHNEIDER

I ought to say—you probably all know it—he was practically tone deaf; he didn't enjoy music at all.

LAMONT

I always got a lot more out of Dewey's books, of course, than his lectures. Like many others I found it hard to concentrate on his drawl. But when I come to his works and look at the massive corpus he produced, I always feel enormously impressed. The only trouble was that, as I told him—and undoubtedly others did too—there was no single book that sort of pulled his whole work or system—if he had a system—together. And I understand that toward the end of his life he did start to work on such a book and had finished about three-quarters of it.

Now the story is that that was lost. He and Mrs. Dewey came back one summer from Nova Scotia—they drove—and pulled up in front of their apartment house at Fifth Avenue and 97th Street. They left their bags with the doorman to bring up, and went upstairs in the elevator. When the doorman had brought up the baggage, Dewey looked around and said to Roberta, "My heavens, my brief case isn't here." Mrs. Dewey immediately rushed downstairs. The brief case *had* been taken out of the car, they knew; but it had disappeared. And in that brief case was the manuscript of Dewey's almost completed book summarizing his whole philosophy.

There was no carbon copy. Perhaps some little boy came in off the street and ran away with the brief case. I think it was a tragedy. I wonder if anybody else has light to throw on that lost manuscript.

FARRELL

I would say that *Experience and Nature* is a fairly complete account of his views.

KALLEN

The only light I would want to throw on it is that I would hold it's not a tragedy.

LAMONT

Oh! Why, Horace!

KALLEN

I think, Corliss, that if you wanted Dewey to state a system, he'd have to contradict himself. He'd have to set up a number of fixed points and a structured order of the universe, and deny practically all the fundamental concepts with which he's identified. He thinks the functional thoughts, and he writes the functional thoughts. And it doesn't matter what field you enter into, his quarrel with the psychologists, and his quarrel with Russell, his quarrel with the neo-realists, all turn on the fact that they want to use rigidities, to deny process.

You remember in *Human Nature and Conduct,* the meaning that he gives habit, which is a key concept there, is such that it's bound to allow for variation and to discard the repetitive rigidities we usually identify with habit. And habit is a foundation of human nature; habit as varying indefinitely, from act to act, is the foundation of practically all interpretations of human nature that Dewey makes, as I see it.

LAMONT

I would still insist that it was a tragedy, Horace, because this book—unlike *Experience and Nature* which was really quite a technical job and couldn't be understood by the average man, let us say—this outline was going to be in more simple language, something like *Reconstruction in Philosophy,* which is a very readable book. And sure, there may have been inconsistencies that would have come out in it, but I think that it was really a great loss.

FARRELL

In *Reconstruction in Philosophy,* Dewey said

that there was one sentence that was central with him all his life. He said, "Growth itself is the only moral end." I mean, he had a feeling constantly of growth.

SCHNEIDER

Woodbridge * used to say that the best statement of Dewey's philosophy was *The Quest for Certainty,* and I think in many ways that's true.

KALLEN

Yes, I quite agree.

GUTMANN

I mentioned to you earlier this evening the remark that Sterling Lamprecht made once that Dewey and Woodbridge had a particularly fruitful influence on one another in the years in which they shared an office. It was *The Quest for Certainty,* I think, that came right after that; and Woodbridge was working—

RANDALL

It was the ten years from about 1916 on to about

---

* Professor F. J. E. Woodbridge taught philosophy at Columbia from 1902 to 1939.

1926, when Dewey's *Experience and Nature* came out.

SCHNEIDER
Yes, it was a whole series of years—

GUTMANN
Yes, except that Woodbridge had another office part of that time as Dean of the Graduate Schools.

RANDALL
That was the time when they had long conversations with each other.

NAGEL
I wonder if anybody could throw some light on Dewey's relations with some of his other colleagues at Columbia. I mean men like Charles Beard * or the economist—

GUTMANN
Simkhovitch?

* Professor Charles A. Beard taught politics at Columbia from 1907 to 1917.

NAGEL

Vladimir Simkhovitch.* I never quite understood just how much intellectual interchange there was between them.

SCHNEIDER

More with Robinson.

RANDALL

Robinson, Simkhovitch, and to some extent Beard. Franz Boas † also was in on that. They would gather and talk for a long while after lunch at the Faculty Club.

NAGEL

Yes, but as far as Boas is concerned, their relations—at least according to the reports I've heard—were one-sided. Dewey got a good deal from Boas; but if one can judge from what former students of Boas repeat, Boas got very little from Dewey. Boas supposedly found a great deal to in-

---

* Professor Vladimir G. Simkhovitch taught economics at Columbia from 1904 to 1942.
† Professor Franz Boas taught anthropology at Columbia from 1899 to 1937.

terest him in Wilhelm Dilthey, but allegedly Dewey did not have much to offer him. I recently heard about a joint seminar that Boas and Dewey gave, which Dewey attended very faithfully. Boas did all the talking, while throughout the semester Dewey didn't say a word. Toward the end of the semester, after a long exposition of some question by Boas, he turned to Dewey and asked, "Professor Dewey, what do you think of this?" Dewey sat for a while lost in thought and finally said, "Well, I don't really know." And that, according to my informant, was Dewey's contribution to the seminar.

LAIDLER

It is interesting that while, as a college lecturer, Dewey may have been somewhat dull at times, he could be very effective at large public gatherings. I remember hearing his quiet but effective denunciation of corruption in city government during the mayoralty campaign of 1929 when he was supporting Norman Thomas for mayor. And I remember his presidential address as head of the League for Industrial Democracy at its 35th Anniversary luncheon in 1940, when he was stirred by Hitler's aggression in Europe. He spoke clearly and eloquently about the need for defending and strengthening democracy at home as well as abroad, through better education for democratic citizenship in our schools and colleges, greater participation of collegians and the general public in political life, and the building up of a more democratic and stable industrial structure. He urged America to look forward, not back, and to learn to create democracy as a living reality in our common life.

And some of us here remember his moving address at the Commodore Hotel at his 90th Birthday Dinner in 1949. There was an audience of over 1500. He was very good in spite of the fact that during the day and early evening he had stomach trouble and was lying in bed for several hours. And when he left home about eight o'clock to come down to the Commodore, his car was held up for an hour on Fifth Avenue by a parade. He came in breathlessly at nine o'clock; but he didn't make any reference to his illness or to the delay. At the end of a long evening of speeches, he spoke without notes, and his address ended with a warning to America against making fear a predominant motivation for its activities, and a call of dedication to the tasks ahead. Everyone was very much moved.

RANDALL

Well, at a public meeting like that he didn't try to think in public. He knew what he wanted to say.

FARRELL

That's not true. His speech at his 90th Birthday which was very simple and very moving was impromptu. I want to make one remark. He said, "Democracy begins in conversation."

And then after he came back from Mexico and the Trotsky hearings he gave a most eloquent speech which was later printed in a pamphlet, *The Truth Is on the March*. That was a wonderful speech, strong, eloquent, moving.

SCHNEIDER

The first public speech I heard of his was a campaign speech for Woodrow Wilson in the old Columbia Commons. That was very vigorous, in a real campaign oratory style.

Dialogue on Dewey

KALLEN

When my sister Deborah came on a propaganda tour from Israel—she was a pre-Dewey Deweyite, so to speak—they had a meeting, dinner, in the Fifth Avenue Hotel where Judge Julian Mack was living. He was a sponsor of the association for the school which my sister was head of in Israel. Dewey came down with Roberta; and he spoke for about 25 minutes and seemed to sum up the entire credo of the progressive view of education in the simplest and most straightforward way I've ever heard him talk. That speech was not recorded, unhappily; but it's one of the best statements from him that I can remember. So occasions will sometimes stir even a reticent man to—

LAIDLER

That's true, and Dewey showed the same ability, at his infrequent appearances, to impress a radio audience. When he spoke in a series of radio discussions on the New Deal over an NBC network in the early Thirties, some reactionary listener from Texas wrote to the station, complaining that John Dewey was one of the two or three who spoke so persuasively in connection with liberal causes that he was one of the most dangerous men in America. This Texan wanted to see him hanged from the nearest lamppost.

KALLEN

There are people other than those in Texas who had that feeling. One summer they were on the farm, I think on Robbie's * farm in Pennsylvania; Dewey had been very ill and had to be hospitalized; and the hospital happened to be a Catholic hospital. Now I'd never heard John before ever say an unkind word about any group; but he was very angry about the sort of treatment that he had had there somewhere in Pittsburgh.

FARRELL

You know it's a very interesting thing—at the end of his life there were a number of unfair attacks on him by Catholics, and they were very nasty. As a matter of fact, John on principle defended the right of parochial schools to exist.

LAMONT

Now that we're on the subject, Dewey also had

* Roberta Dewey, the second Mrs. John Dewey.

a rather nasty time at a Catholic hospital somewhere in Arizona.

SCHNEIDER

He had a very unpleasant incident there. I don't know the details.

JOHNSON

It was in Phoenix, and they hoped they could get a deathbed conversion.

FARRELL

Coming back to growing things, when my son Kevin was young, about a year and a half, John and Roberta came over to see him; and Kevin sat on his lap and pulled John's mustache; and John started talking about Shaw. His criticism was that in Shaw's work it seemed clear that Shaw didn't like growing things and didn't like children. I mention that because again and again one saw that John had a feeling for growing things. He thought of change in terms of growth.

KALLEN

Alvin, weren't a number of parts from *Human*

Nature and Conduct published in *The New Republic*?

JOHNSON
I can't remember.

KALLEN
I had an impression that a number of sections from that—

NAGEL
I think it was *Individualism Old and New* that was first published in *The New Republic*, as a special supplement.

KALLEN
Yes, *Individualism Old and New* abridged—practically all of it.

SCHNEIDER
I think *Human Nature and Conduct* is his best book—the one I like to come back to most.

FARRELL
He wrote, I thought, one of his best pieces after

70 for that *Encyclopedia of Unified Science*. It was a monograph on valuation.

SCHNEIDER

Yes, that was a good essay. He also wrote two excellent articles for Baldwin's *Dictionary of Philosophy*.

KALLEN

Yes, and for Monroe's *Encyclopedia of Education*.

RANDALL

And the *Encyclopedia of the Social Sciences*. There are some extremely good articles in that.

KALLEN

When *The Dial* came to New York—I'd been a contributing editor of *The Dial* while I was out West—and it had been reorganized, we arranged to have Thorstein Veblen and Dewey as contributing editors. It was a unique episode in the history of American journalism.

JOHNSON

Yes. [*Laughter.*]

Dialogue on Dewey

KALLEN

There were three of us, and Dewey had a number of pieces in *The Dial* all dealing with political questions.

FARRELL

Does anyone know about the relations of Dewey and Veblen?

KALLEN

Dewey adopted certain of Veblen's concepts for a while. I know he was very much taken with the notion of conspicuous consumption; he maybe got confirmation for some of his own prejudices; and he spoke of Veblen with maybe more admiration than Alvin has.

JOHNSON

Yes, he wouldn't talk to me about Veblen because, he said, "It's well known that you can never get a Dane to speak fairly about a Norwegian." [*Laughter.*]

GUTMANN

Horace, I think you've told me things about the

New School that belong in the picture—some of his contacts. Was there contact at that time between Dewey and Veblen?

KALLEN
Oh, yes. We used to have long lunches with Robinson presiding and Beard appearing occasionally, and Veblen and an Armenian named Ardzrooni. We were all living in the same New School building; Leo Wolman and Harry Elmer Barnes were also tenants. We were the resident faculty, so to speak. The superintendent had a wife who was an excellent cook; and there would be long lunches with a joining of minds involving different departments in a great variety of ways. I don't know whether we were competing with *The New Republic* lunches or not. I think ours were longer, Alvin.

JOHNSON
I think probably they were.

KALLEN
And Dewey would come down sometimes and not be very vocal, but at that time he gave me the impression of enjoying the situation. And of course

his lectures at the New School in those two years were very well attended indeed.

LAIDLER

Getting back to Dewey's desire for change and growth in individuals and in social and political institutions, I think we saw this in many of his activities after his Columbia teaching career was over. I happened to be on a number of committees with him from the late Twenties on, calling for new political and economic alignments. One was the League for Independent Political Action. He was Chairman of it for about five years; and James H. Maurer, President of the Pennsylvania Federation of Labor, was Vice-chairman. The Committee met frequently in the Advertising Club of New York, with Charney Vladeck as the host; and Dewey took an active part in it. Later, in 1946, when he was 87, he became Honorary Chairman of another organization formed under the chairmanship of A. Philip Randolph, President of the Brotherhood of Sleeping Car Porters, and known as the National Educational Committee for a New Party.

In all of his articles and informal discussions about these committees, Dewey said that, to make democracy really work in these days of complex national and international issues, political parties should present the issues to the electorate in as clear and understandable a way as possible. Too often, he said, they were indulging in evasions and double talk and in irrelevant vote-catching devices, and were leaving the American people utterly confused about real issues and the parties' positions on them. When he joined the Liberal Party in his last years, and became Honorary Vice-chairman, he did it because he thought it was trying to do more than any other party to educate the public.

He was always thinking in terms of something that was new and did not follow the old traditions, but a political pattern that—whether it led to a new party or new movement, or just shocked the old parties—would lead to some alignment that was equipped to meet present crises and the present economic situation better than the old alignment.

FARRELL

When he was 88 or 89 I asked him to write a pamphlet for the United Automobile Workers, CIO, on what the workers should know. He agreed and was going to write it; but things got fouled up in the Education Department of the Auto Workers, and the project was never carried out; but he had agreed immediately that he'd do it.

SCHNEIDER

Do you remember, Mr. Laidler, how he got involved in the People's Lobby? I remember that he defended the People's Lobby theoretically as a very important experiment; and he hoped that a great deal would come out of it. I thought the main factor here was his personal relations to Ben Marsh.

LAIDLER

Yes, I think it was largely because of the personality of Ben Marsh, and Dewey's feeling that Ben was one of the most dedicated, honest and independent spirits in the field of political lobbying; also because of their close agreement on such things as the single tax philosophy, public ownership of public utilities, conservation, and other social issues. He felt that Marsh, despite the Lobby's tiny budget, was an effective force in stirring up national legislators to investigate social abuses and to initiate progressive legislation. He finally resigned from his chairmanship over disagreement regarding Ben's stand on certain international questions, but continued his interest in the Lobby's domestic program.

FARRELL

Two other facts here: One was, he helped found the Teachers Union; the second was that he put aside his work, *Logic,* which meant a great deal to him, and went to Mexico as chairman of the Commission of Inquiry which gave Leon Trotsky the opportunity to answer the charges made against him and his son at the Moscow trials. He did this in the interest of truth and justice. I went down with him. All the way to Mexico he worked. He read completely through the documents. He went to Mexico more or less thinking that Stalin rather than Trotsky was right. On the basis of the evidence that Trotsky presented, plus what Dewey read on the Moscow trials, he came to the conclusion that Trotsky and the other defendants were right. However, he did not agree with Trotsky's political views.

Dewey made a very perceptive remark on Trotsky. He said that it was tragic to see such brilliant native intelligence locked up in absolutes. He returned from Mexico with a strengthened faith in democracy as contrasted with the workings of the Soviet and Fascist dictatorships. I was struck by the seriousness with which he worked. And a small detail: nobody could do anything for him; he wouldn't let you open a door for him. There was a kind of casual independence about him.

RANDALL

Well, it was the same when he analyzed the Sacco-Vanzetti trial.

FARRELL

His analysis of the Sacco-Vanzetti trial was very fine. I was young then. I read it, and thought it was one of the best things written about the case.

LAMONT

This leads me to what I consider an important question: how Dewey ever got the time to do all these things. He was teaching full time; he was continuously writing and producing books and articles; and yet at the same time he was carrying on these extra-philosophical activities, such as the LID, the Trotsky Commission in Mexico, the People's Lobby, the League for Independent Political Action. How did he do it? Did he abolish all his social life?

FARRELL

No. In Key West—

LAMONT

Will somebody tell me how he did it?

FARRELL

In Key West he would get up and have breakfast about eight. He'd work in the morning; he'd eat and take a nap, and then he might work on a puzzle or he'd go bathing. And sometimes in the evening he'd go out to dinner, and occasionally he'd give a cocktail party. Also, of course, he'd read. But he did almost all of his work in Key West in the morning.

RANDALL

Well, for one thing he used to give us the advice —he said, "What you want to be sure to do is to get the reputation of being a very bad man on a committee. Then they won't put you on any university committees." He kept off them.

TAYLOR

People work harder at being bad on committees now than they used to.

GUTMANN

Mr. Laidler made the point that after his retirement from academic life he threw himself into other activities. He had of course been interested and somewhat active, but I think it was amazing how he kept on going in his later years.

KALLEN

Harry, do you know anything about his relation to the women's movements? They were very important in his psyche, as I recall. He was stronger for women's rights than Russell ever was, and on the whole much more effective.

LAIDLER

Well—

RANDALL

Well, I remember that famous suffrage parade in New York. He marched in it.

KALLEN

Yes, he marched in it.

FARRELL

Mead told about Dewey engaging in activities

like that as far back as when he was at the University of Chicago. And of course, John founded the Dewey school there.

KALLEN

Well, he was in close contact with the group around Jane Addams; and I had the impression, after I got West and could escape from Madison to Chicago—and usually it was escape either to the Northwestern Settlement or Hull House—that Jane had a very telling effect on Dewey. There were two or three women in that group.

FARRELL

Well, Jane Addams was a remarkable woman, everybody knows, a fine person—

SCHNEIDER

Yes, she always—

FARRELL

A remarkable person.

GUTMANN

In spite of what was said earlier about Dewey

himself not caring for reminiscences, my impression is that there was one exception to that; and that concerned his relationship to elementary education, schooling in general. I think he talked more about that perhaps because schools remained to some extent a primary concern—and possibly to correct some of the misunderstandings and abuses that were fairly common in the name of a Deweyan education.

FARRELL

A very touching little story about Dewey was in relationship to Edgar Lee Masters. You know, Edgar Lee Masters was very shy; he thought he wasn't liked. In his relations with almost everyone—with Dreiser, Sandburg and others—he felt this way until he got to know them. But then he opened up. He and Dewey met, and they'd sometimes go to dinner together; and it had the greatest meaning for Masters that Dewey liked him. They became warm friends.

And Dewey became a good friend of Carlo Tresca. There was a very funny incident with Tresca. Carlo gave a party one night at his home in Brooklyn. And you know John; he would take a drink, but he wouldn't get drunk or anything like that. Carlo had one of his boys go up to Dewey and say, "Professor, Carlo he say you getta drunk as you want; I taka care of you." And John started smiling and said, "I'm being taken care of." But he liked Carlo very much.

LAIDLER
Also in the early days he took a great liking to Frank Tannenbaum after Frank's advocacy of the IWW program had led to conflict with the law.

SCHNEIDER
I remember one lecture he gave that made a big impression on me. It was a regular lecture in his ethics course; and that day he wasn't having very good luck with the development of his theme. He was trying to analyze the criteria by which you should judge a culture. It was a rather dull lecture, and he knew it; and towards the end of the hour he stopped talking and looked out the window for—I think it must have been as much as two minutes without saying a word. And then he said, "What I mean to say is that the best way to judge a culture is to see what kind of people are in the jails!"

Dialogue on Dewey

FARRELL

Well, I used to see him sometimes on his birthday. On the day before his 80th birthday, I was waiting with him for Robbie to come down; and we were having a drink. He said, "You know, something's happened to me. I don't know what it is— maybe it's the fall of France [this was 1940]. I've been fallow for six months."

LAIDLER

That was the time when he said he had received a lot of very flattering messages from his friends in China and other parts of the world during that birthday period. He said, "I don't believe them, but I lap them up, I lap them up!" He seemed to be quite happy.

SCHNEIDER

I saw one postcard he got from Texas after one of his broadcasts. It said, "This is just to tell you, Mr. Dewey, that you're going straight to hell!" [*Laughter.*]

FARRELL

He had great respect for David Dubinsky and

Walter Reuther, and occasionally he mentioned them. There was one incident which was touching. John wanted a picture of Reuther; he thought that he was a coming statesman. And he wrote a letter to Walter requesting it. But Walter felt, "Well, John Dewey wouldn't want *my* picture; I'd like *his*." Walter never sent the picture. I wrote a letter to Reuther about this, and that's what he told me.

LAIDLER

You heard what Walter said about Dewey as a philosopher and educator at the 90th Birthday Dinner?

FARRELL

Well, there was and still is strong admiration for Dewey among the leaders of the Auto Workers. In fact they put out a pamphlet on him. Some of them feel that they are actually applying Dewey's ideas. This pleased Dewey very much. He definitely influenced their educational work. Among the Auto Workers there were some who felt that Dewey was the greatest living American of our times. They had genuine respect for him.

LAMONT

It's a pity that John Dewey didn't keep letters, as I understand it, or very few. Nor did he keep copies of the ones he wrote. There seem to be very few extant.

FARRELL

He wrote a lot of letters; even when he was old he wrote many letters in longhand, and his handwriting was quiet clear.

RANDALL

Clearer than his typing!

LAMONT

Did you, Jim, ever go to Hubbards in Nova Scotia? Do you know anything about his life there?

FARRELL

No, I was invited to go there one summer, but I couldn't make it. I remember getting a card, a letter; he seemed to have been very happy, and he liked it. You know, it was probably similar to Key West. At Key West he'd go bathing every day.

SCHNEIDER

I spent one weekend on his farm out there in Huntington, Long Island. Mrs. Dewey said, "The house isn't being used this weekend, why don't you go out there?" And gave us the key. "There won't be anybody out there; you can do what you please."

So I got into Dewey's bedroom for the weekend, and I noticed that on one side of the bed was a whole pile of what we used to call dime novels. And in the fireplace was a huge mound of cigarette butts. And I was sort of looking the whole situation over, hadn't been there long, when Evelyn * burst in. *She* wanted to spend the weekend there with some friends of hers. So she said, "You come along; we'll have a little weekend party here; but we'll have to do a little shopping." So she had us get into an old Ford—I remember this quite distinctly because halfway to the store the whole steering wheel came off. She said, "Aw, don't worry; it does that once in a while." And she stuck it right back! [*Laughter.*] It was quite a wild weekend.

LAIDLER

What about the story I've heard—I don't know

* John Dewey's eldest daughter.

whether it's true or not—that he had a number of cows on that farm and used to supply the neighborhood with milk?

SCHNEIDER
No, eggs.

LAIDLER
Eggs. And at one time his man failed to show up, and Dewey went around with eggs; and one person saw him with his baggy trousers and said, "Well, the regular man is not here, but they sent an old man to deliver eggs from the Dewey farm." [*Laughter.*]

FARRELL
There are variations to that. The way I heard it was that he was invited to this rich lady's home; and as he walked in, she said, "Oh, my God! the egg man!"

SCHNEIDER
I think he delivered eggs fairly regularly for a while.

KALLEN
I think you've hit on the origin of *egghead*, haven't you? [*Laughter.*]

Dialogue on Dewey

RANDALL

Well, Tannenbaum has the story that he asked Dewey to come and talk at a meeting of the IWW, and Dewey agreed; and he turned up in evening dress and saw that that wasn't the thing to do so he kept his overcoat on. And out of the pocket of his overcoat there you could see emerging from some paper a beefsteak that he was taking somewhere or other. [*Laughter.*]

LAIDLER

What about Dewey's forgetfulness? I know that one time when he went to a studio where he was scheduled to read his address over a large radio network, he put his hand in one pocket, then in another. "Oh, I've forgotten my speech!" he said in dismay. Well, fortunately we had a carbon copy, and handed it to him, saving the day. But was that typical of Dewey?

THOMAS

I think he was a typical absent-minded professor. I shared a coat closet with him at one time; and one night when I was going home I found in my pocket half a dozen very fine linen handkerchiefs.

So I took them out and left them on his desk. The next morning I found that he had been going to somebody's birthday party and wanted to be so sure that he'd take them that he put them in his coat. Only it was *my* coat. [*Laughter.*]

FARRELL

Incidentally, he never dressed like an old man. He wore tweeds, bright clothes. When he was about 82 I was talking to him about Nicholas Murray Butler. John was older, but he said, "One of the troubles with Nicholas Murray Butler is that he's an old man."

He always wanted to do things for himself; he didn't want to be helped. In the same way, for instance, in Key West, he wouldn't allow his children to help him. The yard was full of boards and nails, and he'd insist on walking there without any help.

LAIDLER

There's another story about his walking with a friend across a college campus, and a little boy coming along and saying, "Would you give me five cents?" Dewey looked down, was a little peeved, put his hand in his pocket and gave a nickel to the boy, and then said to his friend, "The trouble with boys in this city is that they're always asking you for money." The friend looked around and said, "Well, Professor Dewey, isn't that *your* son?" John looked and said, "Why, yes, I guess it is." [*Laughter.*]

SCHNEIDER
I heard the story that in the Michigan days Mrs. Dewey would take the children to the grocery store in a baby buggy, and then she'd walk home with the groceries and forget the baby buggy. So the neighbors would have to bring the children home later on. [*Laughter.*]

FARRELL
One of his most striking traits was his utter simplicity—

VOICE
Yes!

FARRELL
And his directness. I don't think I ever heard him utter a dishonest word, or evade an issue. He

always would answer questions or tell you what he thought. If he didn't know, he would say, "I don't know." Once he said to me, "You know, I made mistakes, but I went on what I knew. That's all I could do." He always seemed to be testing what he thought. But his simplicity—I never in my life met a man with such genuine and overwhelming simplicity.

RANDALL

He remarked once in the early days of this last war—he said, "You know, if I hadn't been so wrong about that First World War, I'd be a lot wronger about this one."

KALLEN

That would sort of contradict his principle of habit, wouldn't it?

RANDALL

Well, that's growth.

KALLEN

No, if he'd be a lot wronger, it would be simply a confirmation of the repetition of the past and intensification—like tobacco habits! [*Laughter.*]

FARRELL

I recall I was arguing with him once around 1941 in Key West at dinner, and he finally burst out at me. He wasn't angry, but he was intense, and his feeling was very real. He said, "Well, I feel this way: I'm an American, and I think we're right."

KALLEN

Well, *Democracy and Education* had a small discussion of war, in which Dewey pointed out that war could further communication and a heightening of contact between peoples.

As to Russia, I know he returned from there with a good deal more sympathy than I had when I returned. And it was the contact with Trotsky and the whole trial business that seemed to have fortified his later attitudes on Russia.

FARRELL

He also wrote—I think it's a very important book for the present—*Democracy and Culture.*

KALLEN

Freedom and Culture.

FARRELL

Freedom and Culture. In the Thirties, after all, the great problem was totalitarianism; we were moving to war; and totalitarianism represented the opposite of everything he believed. And I think it was very consistent that he saw the issues in the Second World War as he did. I think he was right, in defending the war against Hitler.

He also admired Franklin D. Roosevelt. He thought that President Roosevelt had made clear to the American people the issues which involved them and their fate. He felt that this in itself was most important.

I think that one of the things that concerned him, and particularly in relationship to public problems, was the statement of questions so that they could be focussed as a problem, and so that there could be action. That goes back to another book of his for which I have high regard, *The Public and Its Problems.*

KALLEN

I don't have a clear recollection at all of *The Public and Its Problems;* but it seemed to me that it involved two lines of thought which didn't quite meet. On one side, there was the pluralistic conception of a variety of publics; and on the other side, there was the feeling that in any public the individual was a function of the public, and not the public of the individual. And this concept of the individual (as against the feeling for individuality he expressed in relation to his students) always seemed to me to be extremely ambiguous, and not right.

FARRELL

Well, I'll have to reread the book. However, what I have in mind is his account of how a public is created, how a public becomes a public. In my mind, this is why the book has enduring value.

RANDALL

He always regarded that as one of his best books. And he thought it was one of his least appreciated.

SCHNEIDER

It had a curious conclusion, though, along the lines you were saying, as I remember. After all his theoretical analysis of various publics and so on, he comes out with a rather sentimental defense, I think, for what he called "a face-to-face community" in which individuals really know each other face to face as persons. I don't know whether it was Robert MacIver that influenced him or Charles Horton Cooley. Cooley, I guess.

KALLEN

I should say it was his youth in Vermont that influenced him.

SCHNEIDER

It was the old Vermont town-meeting idea and that conception of democracy that seemed to come out on top in his mind.

KALLEN

It came out at the end.

FARRELL

Well, he came back to it in the end. I mean, for instance, the remark on his 90th birthday, "Democracy begins in conversation." Of course, you see, he grew up in a period when relationships were intimate. He practically goes back to the time of town-hall democracy. Later we see him thinking about this whole development of industrial society, about a range of problems that demanded very complicated solutions; and we see his emphasis on scientific method. The sense of the individual was rooted in his thought. And many of his books begin with an emphasis on the functioning individual as a biological and social animal. Again and again he started out that way, as in *Experience and Nature* and his monograph on valuation. The sense of individuality in a community permeates his thinking.

GUTMANN

But does he have any nostalgia at all for this Vermont boyhood? I see no sign of it.

SCHNEIDER

No, he told me he left that God-forsaken country as soon as he could.

RANDALL

Yes, he said, "I don't see why you fellows want to go back to summer places in Vermont. I got out as soon as I could." [*Laughter.*]

As a matter of fact, I think that face-to-face business, while it undoubtedly has overtones of town meetings and so on, that's one of the things he got from Jane Addams.

SCHNEIDER

Well, he *shared* it with Jane Addams. But I think more impressive was his introduction to that reprinting of Jane Addams's book * in which he was concerned with international relations. And after he had taken this outlawry of war very seriously—I remember how earnestly he discussed the theory of that—then he came out on this problem of international relations and said, "The only way to make headway in the international community is to start with the non-political aspects of society—conversation, food, technical meetings, congresses and so on—and end up with politics. But certainly don't start with politics!"

RANDALL

Well, in that he was influenced by Jane Addams.

SCHNEIDER

There's pretty fundamental realism in his own thinking.

* *Peace and Bread*, Columbia University Press, 1945.

TAYLOR

Did any of you have a chance to talk much psychology with Dewey in the latter years of his life? I saw him perhaps every few weeks at his apartment; and at one or two of the sessions we talked about what was going on in the field of psychology. He said at one point that he felt that his own views in philosophy and psychology were much more radical than anything he was reading of the contemporary figures. He found them boring. He made a lot of fun of analytical psychology—clinical psychology—as missing the whole point of the social relationships which were more fully determinant of conduct than anything Freud had to say, and argued a very strongly anti-Freudian position on practically everything. I never heard him sharper or more difficult about any theory than he was about Freud's.

FARRELL

No, he didn't particularly seem to care for Freud. Of course his whole conception of the unconscious was different and was related to his conception of habit. He once wrote that the mind of civilized man resides in the unconscious. But there was an incident which pleased him very much: Dr.

Bruno Bettelheim, who runs the Sonia Shankman Orthogenic School at the University of Chicago, has a Freudian orientation. In his book, *Love Is Not Enough,* which is a classic in its field, he makes an acknowledgment to the ideas of Dewey. Dr. Bettelheim told me that after he'd been analyzed in Vienna, he had read John Dewey, and the influence was lasting. I told that to Dewey, and Dewey was very pleased.

GUTMANN

There's at least one other psychologist whose thought and work combined Freud's teachings and Dewey's. I mean Patrick Mullahy, the author of *Oedipus Myth and Complex.* I met him in the middle Forties through Dewey. He was a student at Columbia where he's now taking a degree with an excellent essay on Dewey. He has taught at Columbia and at Bennington as well as in the William Alanson White Institute. Right now, he is teaching at Hunter. As I said, his work derives from Freud largely in terms of Harry Stack Sullivan's interpretations, but he always acknowledges intellectual as well as personal obligations to Dewey. Did you [*to*

Taylor] mean to say that Dewey expressed specific aversion to Freudian psychology?

TAYLOR
Yes. Any psychology which was introspective, which used theories of the unconscious, he was quite impatient about.

SCHNEIDER
The libido especially.

GUTMANN
Pat Mullahy said to me very much what you [*indicating Farrell*] said before about Dewey's interest in Freud. Specifically, he emphasizes Dewey's positive interest in Freud's theory of repression.

FARRELL
It's interesting because James was one of the first to read Freud and met him when he was in America. James of course also wrote of the unconscious. But Dewey after all was a *social* psychologist, as was Mead. They were concerned with the individual and the self as a product of society. It is

also interesting to mention another Freudian, Dr. Paul Schilder, who wrote a book called *The Image and Appearance of the Human Body*. He studied how the human being creates his own image of himself and of his body; he considered the problem from a neurological, psychiatric and sociological view; and he came to the same conclusions as James, Dewey and Mead, even though he had no use for them.

SCHNEIDER

Well, I think we should talk something about Arthur Bentley here because during Dewey's last years I think his psychology was influenced a great deal by Bentley, and not merely the theory of knowing. The relations between Bentley and Dewey were very close; and some of you may know more about that than I do.

KALLEN

They wrote a book together, *Knowing and the Known*.

LAMONT

Was this really a joint enterprise?

SCHNEIDER

Bentley did most of the writing but, I think, using Dewey's ideas to a large extent.

LAMONT

Coming back to Columbia a minute, Woodbridge and Dewey were both naturalists; they had a similar outlook on the world in that respect; and yet they never seemed intellectually akin. Was that a matter of temperament, or was there really a great difference in their philosophies?

SCHNEIDER

Oh, I'd like to speak of that because I remember very vividly a dinner party that Woodbridge gave, and Dewey was there; and Woodbridge began talking about the visible world and the importance of vision for the theory of understanding. Dewey listened to it all; but then he said rather quietly, "I think this whole problem of understanding should be approached not from the point of view of the eyes, but from the point of view of the hands. It's what we grasp that matters." The next day Woodbridge said to me, "Is Dewey serious about this?" And I said, "Very serious; this is very important to him." He said, "Well, I guess I don't understand this." And I really believe that was the basic contrast in their whole conception of knowledge—Dewey took manipulation very seriously, whereas Woodbridge took the more Platonic visual approach.

LAMONT
Jack, what do you think on that?

RANDALL
Why, there were differences like that, and Dewey took this experimentation very seriously and the manipulation kind of thing. I remember Wendell Bush once remarking, "Woodbridge, he's looking backwards; Woodbridge should have been a bishop. Dewey—Dewey, he lives in a laboratory."

SCHNEIDER
Or a museum.

RANDALL
Well, Bush said a laboratory; there was too much of a museum around it, that was his suggestion.

KALLEN

I guess in both cases experiments would have been performed duly and in good order. [*Laughter.*]

FARRELL

Another incident occurs to me. Immediately after his 90th birthday, I went over and sat in the park with him. He was very frail, but his mind was very good. And he was telling me how he had finally come to the conclusion that he didn't think Einstein was a good philosopher. What he meant was that Einstein was an idealist who assumed that there is pre-established harmony in the universe, and he didn't think that Einstein defended this theory well. And he'd been reading and thinking about Einstein's relationship to philosophy and Einstein's premises, not his scientific conclusions. Needless to say, he had great respect for Einstein and did not attack the theories of relativity. It is clear that he accepted these and integrated them into his philosophical thinking, as is shown, for instance, in *Experience and Nature*. I might add that *Quest for Certainty* could be described as a book which is largely based on the theories of relativity.

Dialogue on Dewey

GUTMANN

I think we ought to say a word about Dewey's personal relations with Professor Montague.* There was less philosophic congeniality there than in the case of Woodbridge and Dewey; but there were obviously, in part in their social outlook and to some extent in their ethics, some points of contact; and there must have been—I don't know the details—a very real friendship.

SCHNEIDER

Well, even intellectually. You remember the meeting of the Philosophy Club in which Montague gave us a lecture on his materialistic theory of conscious energy: the transfer from potential to kinetic energy was the essence of consciousness. And when it came Dewey's turn to comment on that theory, he said, "Well, if you must explain consciousness physically, that seems to me the most sensible theory of consciousness that *I* know. But I would never get interested in that approach to it."

FARRELL

I might remark that Dewey had a very wide

* William Pepperell Montague taught philosophy at Barnard College from 1903 to 1947.

range of friends, of contacts. He went far beyond the academic world. He must have had thousands upon thousands of contacts with people in all ranges of life, from the simplest to the level of statesmen, other philosophers and educators. And it more or less fits his personality that he had so many contacts. After all, he was fundamentally interested in the human being, in the individual, in people. And he had great tolerance of people. His ability to listen was one of his most striking characteristics.

KALLEN

Regarding your questions about psychology, Harold, I recall that Dewey had written a study of the use of language by small children very early in his career; it was a straight psychological inquiry.* I forget when that was published. And of course there was his own psychology which goes back, I think, to the Nineties.

It began as psychology with a soul. And Dewey's abandonment of the soul should be epic. The replacement of the soul by the body under the influence of George Herbert Mead (more of Mead than perhaps of anybody else); the replacement of God

---
* "The Psychology of Infant Language," 1894.

by ideals under the influence of Edward Scribner Ames of Chicago—

SCHNEIDER

Well, you remember, Mr. Kallen, how seriously Dewey took his essay on James, "The Disappearance of the Subject in James." He thought he had a real point on James there, and that was his own tendency.

FARRELL

I think that of course the influence of Mead— it was a very mutual thing. Mead, not Dewey, was the man influenced by Charles Horton Cooley. I mean that one of Mead's starting points was Cooley's conception of "the looking glass self."

SCHNEIDER

Mead stayed closer to Cooley; but Dewey told me he owed a lot to Cooley. And curiously enough, he gave me his copy of Elisha Mulford's *The Nation*. And he said, "In my youth this was a great book." That was, you know, a rationale of the Christian Hegelianism of Frederick D. Maurice. And he said, "We took this very seriously."

KALLEN

Well, it's quite apparent that if you're going to have mind in any sense as a function of body, Mead's account of it would be persuasive, practically compelling. It seems to me especially so since Mead didn't write at all. Anyway the whole record from Michigan on, the whole record of intercommunication, contact, means that Dewey translated what he had heard from Mead and agreed to, into his own special language.

FARRELL

There were two problems which Mead seems to have given more thought to than Dewey. One was the self and communication, and the other was the process of time—the past and the present and the future in the universe, and the general processes of the universe. And also, Mead was interested in the history of philosophy. Lecture notes of Mead's were assembled and published in his book, *Movements of Thought in the Nineteenth Century*, and this would make an excellent textbook. But in their thinking the two men coalesced. I don't know what personal papers Mead left, but if anybody could get at these papers, I think a very fascinating study could be made of the friendship and relationship of the two men.

KALLEN

Well, Jim, I don't know what can be done because Mead's utterance was all in lectures, not primarily written by Mead for publication; it was worked over by Charles Morris and others; and there's no residue. Yet you can read Mead in Dewey; but you cannot read Dewey in Mead. At least I can't.

FARRELL

Well, that's true. One essay in which Mead fully stated his views was "The Genesis of the Self and Social Control." Then there's a second essay, which was printed in the *International Journal of Ethics* in 1925, "On the Nature of an Aesthetic Experience." Mead really thought out and wrote these essays. The thinking in them is very close to Dewey.

SCHNEIDER

Well, I think Mr. Farrell's right about one point especially, that Mead's interest in cosmology and the theory of the present—for instance, in *The Philosophy of the Present*—Dewey didn't share much.

FARRELL

Mead at the end of his life was seriously interested in the thinking of Bergson and Whitehead and was working on their ideas. I don't think Dewey had much interest in Bergson, but Mead had a profound interest in him.

RANDALL

Dewey wrote a very eulogistic introduction to a bibliography of Bergson when Bergson first came over here.

FARRELL

Then I'm wrong.

SCHNEIDER

Dewey's historical work—I observed him pretty carefully when he would expound an historical figure in his class, in the classroom. He always tried to make an individual thoroughly intelligible in terms of his environment. He didn't talk about historical movements or anything of the sort, but he'd make this man seem like a very sensible person in terms of his environment.

KALLEN

No. That's the way Mead functioned.

FARRELL

Of course Dewey was a very good polemicist. Some of his best writing was polemical.

GUTMANN

Didn't that sometimes get in the way of his historical presentation? Even in *Reconstruction in Philosophy*, which I think comes closest to being the kind of summary book you were after before, Corliss. In his treatment of classical philosophers sometimes he was—

FARRELL

He was concerned with advancing the view which was non-traditional. He was concerned not so much with history; he was concerned in the present with what he considered a new view that was more or less all-embracing. I mean that's why there was so much polemics on his part.

LAMONT

You know, during the last few years we've had

this renewed attack on Dewey's educational views, and answers and counterattacks. I wonder how that's coming out? What led to this renewal of an attack? Have you got the answer there, Dr. Taylor?

TAYLOR

Well, I think it's a pretty complex set of factors that make up the reasons for the attacks, some of them being the effect of overpopulation as far as the school system itself is concerned, and a great many practical problems being solved badly and the solutions being blamed on progressives. As much as anything this is part of it. Another aspect is one of the things that bothered Dewey. He spoke of it many times I'm sure to many of you people: the misinterpretation of what he was trying to do by so many of his followers and people who substituted a form of intellectual laziness for the rigor of thought which he was demanding in his theory and practice. I think the combination of very difficult educational situations for the country along with misconceptions of what it was Dewey was really asking us to do, accounts for a good deal of the attack.

Then there has been an over-all stiffening of the

country's mind and attitude to all reform movements and to social change, so much so that any philosophy which advocates social change as an aspect of education and central to it arouses its own resistance. As to how it's coming out, I think that Dewey's ideas are now being smuggled in under such terms as "the necessity for individual development," "attention to the gifted," "more attention to the variety of possibilities in the young," "more guidance, more counseling." These are ideas which go naturally with a flexible plan for education which uses a curriculum adapted to students rather than putting everybody through the same academic program.

In terms of movements towards greater equality of education, and the social philosophy implicit in Dewey's educational theory, things are not going so well. The implication of people like Admiral Rickover * is that to be attentive and patient and kind with students and to deal with them in their various stages of readiness and to mount individual programs of education suited to the level that the students are ready for—this is considered to be sloppy

* Vice Admiral Hyman G. Rickover, author of *Education and Freedom*.

progressivism. On the whole I think the public feels that any program which is an effort to deal directly with the present state of a child's development is somehow loose, sloppy and dangerous for our moral fibre. A Rickover just now will gain much more attention and consent, in the total sense, than anyone who speaks from a point of view more directly in line with John Dewey's thinking.

FARRELL

May I make a comment? You know John Dewey wrote *School and Society* in 1898; and he was concerned with the child in society; he was concerned with co-operative work; knowledge was regarded as a co-operative enterprise that had the character of work. Now at the present time we have a society that is oriented towards leisure; and I believe people fail to recognize the difference between that fact and Dewey's emphasis on co-operation for work and for growth, for the creation of a moral citizen in a democracy. Dewey as an educational thinker insisted that the inner impulse of the child be stimulated. But now, you see, we have mixed all that up with notions of leisure; and I think that a great mistake is being made in what Dewey was really getting at and what is the character of the present, how there is an application today in terms of a leisure society.

KALLEN

Jim, I don't think that the antithesis of leisure and labor would affect Dewey's conception of education. What he was concerned with was essentially the pattern, the detailed pattern of growth and the techniques by means of which it could be facilitated. Now what's entertaining and perhaps ironic is the fact that a good deal of what is called "progressive education" is not postulated on measurements—of IQ's, attitudes, aptitudes and so on. Dewey had no use for measurement. He thought that it was usually a way of stopping growth rather than of facilitating growth.

And his conception of the educative process had been one in which fundamentally you liberated powers by setting tasks; you didn't isolate the object that a child was interested in from the activity which realized the interest. The whole atomic conception of units of attention was something that he disliked. Well now, Rickover would be one of the guys who would use a quantitative sieve and then educate those it had selected by means of a kind of Platonic engineering. And what would the upshot be? As against the feeling for fluidity and flexibility in the person, which to Dewey was the important factor in education, it splits the individual into a creature of labor or leisure. Dewey was concerned with the whole man.

TAYLOR

Well, I think one could go on from there, Horace, to say that in the contemporary situation the rejection of progressive thinking about education has itself been falsely interpreted, in that so many of the things which educators now want to do and are looking for reasons to do, are in fact going back to Dewey's basic insight of adapting a curriculum to individual students. I think that in the total effect of public talk about education there's more conservative talk which is believed than there is progressive thinking on any cultural or economic or social matters of which education is a part.

I think that there's a concealed Deweyism in a great deal of what's being said in criticism of the educational system. The arts just now, I find, are talked about more than ever before and are advocated as educational instruments in the schools in a way in which they never were before. Even the colleges, the last place where progressive ideas creep in, are finding that, in order to meet deeply felt student needs, theatre, music, dance, painting, sculpture are being put into the curriculum. Now the creative arts are all central to the progressive movement and are now not being argued on the same grounds that John argued them, but are being argued because now America—and this is, I think, interesting—they're being argued because now America has to show the world that it too is cultured; therefore let's have our children do more than just play in bands. We want them also to have stringed instruments, which is another way of justifying an educational program in terms of stated ends. There's no longer as much discussion of the means determining ends and of ends being adapted to means. The relationship of means and ends has been lost in all the discussion, so that there are stated ends for education connected with the national interest; and then it is said that the educational system must be adapted to these ends. Now that, I think, is in strongest opposition to Dewey's ideas.

GUTMANN

No, I think there's one stronger; and you've omitted it altogether, I'm surprised to say, and that is the attack on Dewey as the instrument of irreligion.

FARRELL

There's this though: Some of those who attack Dewey as irreligious talk too big about tradition. They talk as though prior to the reforms of Dewey there had been a very good general educational system throughout America; and I think if you go back to *The Hoosier Schoolmaster* by Eggleston, or if you take a fresh look at McGuffey's *Reader,* and if you consider the actual conditions in popular education in the 19th century, you can readily grasp the enormity of the unfairness of the attacks on Dewey. Even if they were right in their current attacks, they're calling up a nonexistent past—there was *no such past* that they can rely on as traditional—there was no good, broad and popular educational system. We had a very bad, a rotten and dangerous popular educational system when John Dewey wrote *School and Society* in 1898. Some of Dewey's critics are completely deforming the past.

RANDALL

On the other hand, in secondary education we had a very much more highly selective elite which was—

FARRELL

Except for the elite, yes. But Dewey wasn't thinking of the elite.

RANDALL

Oh, that wasn't a tribute to the quality of the education—

FARRELL

No.

LAMONT

Dr. Johnson, did you have a comment here?

JOHNSON

I hadn't. This is a field in which I don't know Dewey's work very well. But my own impression of course has been that the attack on Dewey was not only because of his irreligion, so-called, but because of his fundamental radicalism, political radicalism, that the Deweyan education supposedly produces—a kind of intellectual delinquency.

FARRELL

One of the ironies is this. People who do not believe in freedom, people who believe in locking up the mind of the human being, have attacked Dewey as a totalitarian. The reason they've done it is that they say unless you believe in religion, or unless you believe in God, you're totalitarian. This whole business of attacking people of democratic views on the basis of Godless atheism, materialism, totalitarianism, is often done by people who don't want anybody to be free. They're as free as they want to be, which is not very free; so everybody should be like them. And it's vicious and unfair.

KALLEN

They're the same people who say democracy is totalitarian.

FARRELL

Yes, that's what they say.

SCHNEIDER

Well, Dewey really had a very deep resentment

against standardization of all sorts; and I think many people thought that for that reason he was against standards, and every once in a while he spoke that way. I remember once when he was presiding at an educational evening in Teachers College, there was a series of papers on mental testing. And it was all on norms and so on. And at the end of the meeting—I have to tell this story just for the record—at the end of the evening he said, "Listening to these papers I was reminded of the way we used to weigh hogs on the farm. We would put a plank in between the rails of the fence, put the hog on one end of the plank and then pile the other end of the plank with rocks until the rocks balanced the hog. Then we took the hog off; and then we guessed the weight of the rocks!" [*Laughter.*]

KALLEN

Alvin, did you and Dewey ever talk about adult education?

JOHNSON

Not much. He hadn't a consistent view of adult education. Sometimes he had the opinion that adults are after all children; and what applies to children applies to adults; and as with children, you have to spar around until you find that particular point in the child's mind that has the germ of growth. So too with adults. He had very little use for those early notions that we had to develop specific types of teaching for adults. With the adult it is of overwhelming importance that the teacher believe what he has to say; that if the teacher has a passion for it, you might catch the adult that way.

Then at other times he thought that adult education was a kind of misnomer; it was a way of spending time. He'd lose his interest in it entirely.

LAMONT

Of course, Dr. Johnson, what you said about Dewey being considered a radical, and that that was a major factor in the attack on his educational views, is quite true. He *did* believe in socialism; that's one reason he was in the LID. Was he Honorary Chairman or Chairman?

LAIDLER

Well, he was President for a while, and then Honorary President until his death. He was an ardent believer in the aim of the LID, that of educating for increasing democracy in our economic, political and cultural life.

LAMONT

I don't know how much Dewey's belief in socialism really functioned, or how many people even knew he believed in a socialist economy.

FARRELL

It came late in life. He didn't believe in a socialist economy in the sense of a fixed economy. In *Freedom and Culture* you can see that clearly. *Freedom and Culture* represents a later stage of his thinking. He didn't pay as much attention to economics as to other fields.

KALLEN

I wouldn't be disposed to attribute any *ism* to him.

FARRELL

No *isms,* no.

KALLEN

I would say that he was willing to affirm any hypothesis which would enhance the liberation or the growth of people. And his notion about the collective operations of utilities and his critique of the money system, his conception of war—all turn on his faith in the liberation of people, in growth. It went with his whole philosophy of education.

LAIDLER
Dewey thought in terms of democratic socialism, but he was experimental all the way and would have liked to see, say, public ownership of one industry and if that succeeded, go on to other industries. He was pretty near in his thinking to some sort of mixed system, with the retention of a private sector in our economy. With democratic socialists, he insisted upon the strengthening of civil liberties, and contended that public and co-operative ownership was not an end in itself, but a means to enriching the lives of all the people.

SCHNEIDER
He was quite interested in guild socialism, wasn't he?

LAIDLER
Yes.

RANDALL

He had a good many ideas that have been called syndicalistic.

TAYLOR

Well, there's another basic approach, Harry, which I found him taking in conversation about contemporary politics; and that was the impact of modern industrial society and technology on all social forms. I think that in a sense his pragmatism, his instrumentalism, led him towards any solution of a mass problem which could take account of the impact of an industrial society on collective organization. Therefore, as an economic system working fairly for the population he would want distribution ordered not by a process of power groups juggling the needs of the population and exploiting it, but by handling an industrialized society with control by the people over distribution and production. It seems to me that's the way he moves into his political theory and why he was so eloquent and forceful in the LID, because he felt this impulse for having a control of natural and social resources in the hands of the people.

KALLEN

He would question whether the new individualism that's to follow the old could be equated to socialism in his *Individualism Old and New*.

RANDALL

Well, he was quite—very critical, especially at the beginning of the New Deal, of course; and he would say that the part which appealed to him most was Wallace's agricultural program because that had all these local organizations bound up with it, and they in their turn got a lot of Dewey's educational ideas into the program. That's the kind of thing that he liked, wanted to see. What he didn't like was anything like a centralized administration on top. He wanted the participation of—

LAIDLER

He would have liked to see a society that provided economic security, high living standards and equality of opportunity; and to the extent that it was necessary to go forward to some sort of democratic collectivization in order to achieve these ends, why he was willing to go ahead.

RANDALL

Well, that kind of local, regional, decentralized thing is what appealed to him.

KALLEN

That has certain analogies with the guild idea.

RANDALL

Yes.

KALLEN

And after the First World War when the guild movement in England had become important, he had a good deal of interest in that.

FARRELL

Two years ago I was in an Arab village on the frontier of Israel and Jordan; and I met an Arab schoolteacher who knew of Dewey. I must say, Dewey's influence in a number of countries is very important. It's interesting; in Europe he never had great influence.

LAIDLER

He got a tremendous number of messages from

Pakistan, interestingly enough, on the 90th Anniversary, and from India, Japan and other Asian countries.

SCHNEIDER
Dewey's influence is taking hold now, though, in Europe.

FARRELL
Well, then it's new—

SCHNEIDER
Very genuine.

RANDALL
There's a very great interest in Dewey in Italy now.

FARRELL
There is?

SCHNEIDER
And in Germany.

KALLEN
There's a great renewal in Japan.

FARRELL
Japan?

SCHNEIDER
Yes.

THOMAS
Lots of translations going on all the time. We acquired about twenty new ones in the Columbia Library recently.

KALLEN
Well, translations are—transubstantiation.

TAYLOR
The Europeans seem to me to be terribly parochial about Dewey and American philosophy. I know the people around the British universities in the Thirties were reading Dilthey and finding Deweyan things in him that interested them, and then denying any interest in Dewey's pragmatism, so much of which is also to be found in Dilthey.

LAIDLER
The universities of Scandinavia and of other

countries on the Continent seemed to respond more warmly on Dewey's 90th Anniversary than those in Great Britain.

TAYLOR

But even on the Continent the Europeans would praise Dilthey and some of the ideas developed in pragmatism while remaining ignorant of what Dewey was writing. Also some of the analytical philosophers were developing a theory of language which was pure pragmatism, but they just refused to read any Dewey, even the *Logic*. You know, "Who is *he*? An American." [*Laughter.*]

SCHNEIDER

Well, the prejudices, I usually found, they just took for granted. It was in all the books, it must be so, that pragmatism is the ideology of capitalism, and—

TAYLOR
Yes. Yes.

SCHNEIDER
Certain people take it for granted even in James.

Dialogue on Dewey

LAMONT

Mr. Jesse Gordon * had a word on Dewey and socialism. Didn't you say he wrote you a letter?

GORDON

Yes. I wrote something in the middle Thirties about democracy and capitalism and youth in the country during the New Deal period; and I got a letter, to my surprise, from Dewey on Columbia stationery, in which he said, "I'd like to take exception to two things in what you have recently written. You said democracy is based on capitalism. That is untrue. Secondly, you grouped socialism together with fascism and communism; and I don't believe that's quite candid." Signed, John Dewey.

FARRELL

He could write that sort of thing; he could be very much to the point. He sometimes had a neat way of clinching an argument in a few sentences.

GORDON

He was about 75 at that time—and I was un-

* Mr. Gordon, a New York public relations counselor, recorded the Dewey *Dialogue* on tape.

known to him—yet he would take up his pen to write to a stranger.

FARRELL
Yes, he always did that. And, you know, he had a great deal of interest in everything around him. He had a curious mind.

KALLEN
Well, didn't he call logic a theory of inquiry?

FARRELL
John actually lived his philosophy; he really lived his ideas. In that sense he was quite consistent. There's no break or division that I know of between what he wrote and thought and the way he lived, the way he functioned in his relationships with others.

SCHNEIDER
I heard him say once in a very small group—they were pestering him about his educational career; they said, "Wouldn't you say something about your career as an educator?" And he got peeved, and he said, "I'm not an educator; I'm just a philosopher." I don't think he really cared much about being called a teacher.

TAYLOR

Yes, that's true. I've heard him say something like that in a different context. I remember once a great fuss was being made over him as an educator, a social thinker, a man of his time and so on. He said what he was fond of saying, "Sorry, I'm just a philosopher; I'm just trying to think; that's all I'm doing."

SCHNEIDER

The only time I ever heard him speak sharply and really unkindly to a student was once in a seminar. A student was bringing in a report and said rather casually, "I believe this was due to laziness." And Dewey stopped him right there. He said, "Don't you ever talk like that in this seminar! I won't stand for such lazy analysis! Never say, 'This is due to an abstraction!'" [*Laughter.*] Really, he was quite excited; he talked in anger.

KALLEN

Was it an abstraction to get him to know that laziness is an abstraction? [*Laughter.*]

RANDALL

You think it's one of these habits?

KALLEN
I suspect.

LAMONT
Well, it's 11 o'clock and I guess we've about covered the ground.

CHORUS OF VOICES
Oh, no!

GUTMANN
We didn't even—

LAMONT
Let's keep on going, by all means! And incidentally, please remember there are drinks in the other room.

FARRELL
There's one touching incident. One of the last times I saw John I went to have dinner with him and the children and Robbie. We went to a Chinese restaurant with a Chinese couple; the young man had been influenced by John's writings. He was going

back to China to teach Deweyism. John sort of felt that he might endanger his life. John was really very touched, and tried to convince the young Chinese not to go back.

Dewey maintained his Chinese contacts all his life. And I think you all know he was a very good friend of Hu Shih.

KALLEN

Hu Shih brought him a medal from Taiwan some years ago, some kind of what-do-you-call-it? A modern Knight of the Garter business.

SCHNEIDER

Nobody's mentioned his trip to Turkey, and I remember when he came back from his trip to Turkey he seemed to me very much impressed by what he saw there. I think that was the turning point in some of his political thinking.

KALLEN

I recall he had a very definite impact on the educational program of the Turkish Government. And the editor of the chief Turkish paper, who I think is now in disgrace, was here during the World's Fair that we had in the Thirties. I saw something of him with Dewey, and he apparently had been a student at Columbia and had taken courses with Dewey and had become very devoted to him. And he talked about the role of Dewey's theories of education in Turkey. I never got to any details; but Turkey, Japan, China, Mexico, Israel, are all places where the Dewey conception of education is alive. I don't know how much impact it's had, but it's definitely planted and is alive.

FARRELL

It's apparently had a strong impact in Japan because there's been a revival of interest in Dewey. There's a new interest in him in Japan now.

KALLEN

Well, I think most of us have met the current translator, and some of us may have received not only catalogues of his orchids, but also copies of his translations in Japanese.

LAMONT

Oh, you mean Professor Yoshio Nagano, who was John Dewey visiting lecturer in philosophy at

Columbia last year. I think he was from the University of Hiroshima.

FARRELL

It occurs to me there was another member of the Chicago School whom we haven't mentioned and whom Dewey respected very much—Tufts.

LAMONT

James H. Tufts. Dewey did a book on ethics with Tufts.

FARRELL

It was used as a textbook for years. But apparently Dewey and Tufts were very close too.

SCHNEIDER

Yes, very.

GUTMANN

You put that in the past tense, Mr. Farrell—it *still* is a good book.

FARRELL

Oh, is it still used?

KALLEN
Oh, yes.

FARRELL
I studied it. That was the first of my introduction to Dewey, the *Ethics* of Dewey and Tufts. My teacher was E. A. Burtt.

LAMONT
Well, Edwin Burtt was a very good teacher; and you had a very good book.

SCHNEIDER
Yes, but somebody should get a Ph.D. for comparing the second edition with the first. I don't think anybody's done that; and Dewey made some radical changes.

RANDALL
Very radical changes, yes.

LAMONT
Well, can't you arrange that at Columbia?

SCHNEIDER
Somebody else should do that, yes; it's a good,

easy job. [*Laughter.*] You certainly would learn something about Dewey's development.

FARRELL

Yes, certainly the influence he wielded through his ideas and books was very great. But it's very clear; he touched and affected an unusually large number of people in his personal contacts. I should say he met more people, more varieties of people, than almost any philosopher.

TAYLOR

That's true.

FARRELL

And there are always all sorts of stories cropping up about Dewey. There's a New York policeman whom Mrs. Dewey met who's been studying John Dewey's philosophy. And there are all sorts of little incidents of somebody who met Dewey, somebody who wrote him a letter, people way outside the realm of philosophy. I would say that when all his papers and records are collected, you'll find that thousands upon thousands of people were personally touched by John Dewey.

GUTMANN

I think that's true; but I think it's unnecessary to put it in an absolute sense that he had more such influence than any other philosopher. I think that is the kind of pietism that some of us—

FARRELL

I didn't—I didn't mean—

GUTMANN

I have nothing against piety, and I think this has been a very worth-while and *pious* evening; but there's a kind of piety that we would all disparage. You get a certain amount of sentimentalism in that and a certain amount of inaccuracy.

FARRELL

I don't mean pietistic—

GUTMANN

I don't mean to quarrel with you at all—

FARRELL

It just occurred to me that he touched the lives of a great many people. That's all I wish to stress.

RANDALL

That was true of William James also.

SCHNEIDER

Dewey liked a non-academic atmosphere much better than any other philosopher that I know.

LAIDLER

Yes, in the last years of his life, when he was Honorary Vice-chairman of the Liberal Party of New York, he often attended their annual dinners at the Hotel Commodore and seemed to enjoy mingling with the labor and liberal leaders present. There'd be 1500 or so people there; he would get up —he'd be on the dais—and everybody would rise and cheer and so forth. The trade union movement and the general liberal movement—Dewey got a great kick out of them.

KALLEN

Well, you can say that in his own way, which was very different from William James's way, he liked people; and yet his communication with people, direct, personal, was in behavior quite inhibited. When he wrote, it seemed to me he was very much freer. And it seems to me, too, that there was a change after the first Mrs. Dewey died; it seemed to me there was a change in style and a certain increase in outgoingness. I think that the family circle held him pretty tight, distinctly tighter when Mrs. Dewey was alive.

FARRELL

Well, in his last years I often found him outgoing. He'd always ask personal questions, such as, "How are your children?" and things like that. I didn't find so much inhibition there.

LAIDLER

It was interesting to see in the latter part of his life the affection he showed for his small adopted children and the affection they showed him. He never seemed annoyed when they were buzzing around him as he was typing some important article or letter. These adopted children, who had come from war-stricken Europe, found it difficult in those years to know what to call their new ninety-year-old father. One of them said about the time of my visit: "I am a good girl; my sister is a good sister. My mother is a good mother. My *grandfather* is a good grandfather." [*Laughter.*]

FARRELL
That's John.

JOHNSON
I don't think John Dewey ever had anything but a completely democratic relation with children. He used to tell about—this was when he first came to Columbia—he had returned to the apartment and the children had produced a flood in the bathroom, and they were trying to cope with the water. John Dewey was a little—well, he was pretty much—bewildered by it. And one of them said, "Don't stand there like a fool, John. Get a broom and help!" [*Laughter.*]

TAYLOR
I'm afraid I have to run.

LAMONT
I want to ask Horace Kallen a final question; I've been keeping it back all evening. You know, when we were talking about Santayana last fall here, you said that how long a philosopher endures in influence and human memory is really an accident. Now, are you willing to say that with Dewey?

Because here you have not only his philosophy, which I think is going to endure, but his work as an educator. That is, *two* main lines.

KALLEN

What's likely to happen—which is what's happened with churches, Corliss—somebody has to carry on the tradition. You get bored. Now Harold tells how the whole thing has been broken up in relation to Dewey's theories of education; and it may be that the changing scene will be such that Dewey may be tangent to the patterns of the community and what they want for their children through the schools, and the educational system of which it's all a part.

On the other hand, Dewey's thought may be sustained like the Catholic system, which is sustained and diversified as it goes on. The parochial school in 1958 is in no way like the parochial school in 1900. There have been modifications and conflicts; and even any Dewey school will be transformed, and the literature likely to be dropped or reinterpreted or reconstructed, and Dewey would turn in his grave at some of the reconstructions. Or his educational theory may be sustained if there's a party and an organized movement to carry it on. But intrinsically, it's neutral.

It has to be relevant to somebody's passion. Somebody's got to take it up and be willing to live for it and fight for it and die for it and so on—the way it is with all causes. And so with a school program, most certainly, and even more so with a philosophical system, if Dewey can be said to have a system; and it can be said, although the word *system* doesn't seem to me properly to apply. But I don't see that—except as people will turn to the books of a library and except as they're preserved in libraries, like the Bible or anything else—there is any inevitable immortality.

RANDALL
They're preserved now in paperbacks.

KALLEN
You say *preserved*? or pickled?

LAMONT
I am afraid we have to break up finally. I hate to stop this conversation; but I wanted just to read in conclusion a statement made by a gentleman here

on John Dewey's 90th birthday. I haven't got his permission, but I'm going to read it anyway.

"To John Dewey, latest of the great Greek philosophers:

"But have you not been fighting the Greek philosophers? So you have: Greek philosopher has fought Greek philosopher since before Thales and Heraclitus the Obscure. But in one thing you, John Dewey, and the Greeks are one. You have all fought Fear.

"Fear, not of the tiger in the bush, whom man can meet with good spear or repeating rifle. Not of the hostile armies that can be defeated by armies. But vague fears of the night, the starless black night when ghosts walk; the blacker night of the mind, where habits, traditions, abstractions, assumptions, prejudices, hatreds at large, dance a Walpurgis night dance over the prostrate soul of man.

"You, John Dewey and your fellow Greek philosophers are the supreme exorcists of fear. One who has sat at your Greek feet fears not the lurking demon, the malevolent spirit of the men of other ideas, the alleged corruption of morals, the vast bogeys of ideologies. Your followers accept with gratitude the green earth under the wide blue sky, fearing nothing, least of all death, the one opiate of the people.

"Life is sweet, sweeter because of you, John Dewey. Life is significant, more significant because of you, John Dewey. Life is brave because of you.

"Ninety years have stood between you and immortality. Ninety times ninety will go by before men can think of forgetting John Dewey. And then they will have a second thought. Who taught them to live without fears that have no ground? And John Dewey will live for them yet again.

"With the deepest homage of

ALVIN JOHNSON."

JOHNSON
I still agree with that.

BIOGRAPHICAL NOTES

JAMES T. FARRELL was not yet thirty when his place in American literature was established with the publication of the *Studs Lonigan* trilogy. At that time there were some who classified him as a "naturalistic" writer dealing only with slums, rough poverty-stricken people and "lost" adolescents. Few critics knew that Farrell had been a brilliant scholar at the University of Chicago for three years, but decided to leave the university in order to devote himself to writing.

In the field of philosophy he read James, Mead, Tufts and other pragmatists. In 1929, he started to read Dewey, who became one of the great influences in his life and work. In spite of the views of many American critics, the philosophical concept that has permeated Farrell's work since 1929 is not crude materialism; rather it is based on the ideas of society and the individual held by Dewey, Mead and James, and on the idea that character and environment influence each other.

Born in Chicago in 1904, Farrell has published 32 books, including novels, collections of short stories and essays, and is currently at work on a series of novels which he considers the culmination of his life work.

JAMES GUTMANN, Professor of Philosophy and Chairman of the Department of Philosophy at Columbia University, was born in New York City 62 years ago. He was educated at the Ethical Culture School, Columbia College (A.B.) and Columbia University (M.A., Ph.D.). From 1917 to 1928 he taught history and ethics in the Ethical Culture School at New York City, and during that period was managing editor of the *Ethical Standard* and associate leader of the New York Society for Ethical Culture.

A member of the Department of Philosophy of Columbia University since 1920, he is the author of *Schelling—Of Human Freedom* and *Spinoza's Ethics,* and is co-author of other books, including *An Introduction to Reflective Thinking, A College Program in Action,* and *The Philosophy of Ernst Cassirer.*

Biographical Notes

ALVIN SAUNDERS JOHNSON took his A.B. at the University of Nebraska in 1897. The following year, serving as teaching fellow in Greek, he received his master's degree on a study of the political attitude of Euripides. Six months in the Spanish-American War diverted him from classics to the political sciences. He studied at Columbia from 1898 to 1901, and began teaching there in 1902. At this time he first came into contact with John Dewey, a contact that was to grow closer with the years.

After 1906 Johnson served successively as professor in the Universities of Nebraska, Texas, Chicago, Stanford and Cornell. In 1917 he joined the editorial staff of the *New Republic*, where he renewed contact with John Dewey, a valued contributor, a frequent guest at *New Republic* luncheons and the main philosophic influence on *New Republic* policy.

In 1919 Alvin Johnson, together with Charles A. Beard, James Harvey Robinson, John Dewey and other scholars, planned a new type of higher educational institution, which came to be the New School for Social Research. Although Dewey remained on the Columbia Faculty he gave outstanding courses at the New School and remained its revered friend to the end of his life. In the third year of the New School Alvin Johnson became head of the institution. He retired in 1945 to become President Emeritus. Under Johnson's leadership the New School developed a steadily growing following. His most notable achievement was to found the "University in Exile," a faculty manned by distinguished German professors proscribed by Hitler.

Outside the educational field Alvin Johnson's activities have been mainly editorial. He was political science editor for the *New International Encyclopedia* and associate editor of the *Encyclopedia of the Social Sciences*. Among journals, he was associate editor of the *Political Science Quarterly*, and editor of *Social Research*. Most of his writing is unsigned, but he has published a textbook on economics, two novels, three collections of essays and an autobiography, *Pioneer's Progress*.

HORACE M. KALLEN, A.B., Ph.D., L.H.D., Litt.D., was born in Germany in 1882 and came to the United States in 1887. He was educated at Harvard, Princeton, Oxford and Paris.

Biographical Notes

He was a favorite pupil of William James who left his unfinished *Some Problems of Philosophy* for Dr. Kallen to edit, and was in close contact during his service at Harvard with Santayana and Royce. He was an associate of John Dewey and F. C. S. Schiller in developing the pragmatic philosophy with which they are identified. His special interest was extending this philosophy to the arts, to education, and to religion.

His published works include *William James and Henri Bergson, The Liberal Spirit, Cultural Pluralism and the American Idea, Secularism Is the Will of God, Utopians at Bay,* and other books.

Now Professor Emeritus in the Graduate Faculty and Research Professor in Social Philosophy at the New School for Social Research, he also is Honorary President of the Conference on Methods in Philosophy, succeeding the late John Dewey.

HARRY W. LAIDLER, author, economist and Executive Director Emeritus of the League for Industrial Democracy (LID), was born in Brooklyn, N.Y., February 18, 1884. He was educated at Wesleyan

Biographical Notes

University (Conn.), Brooklyn Law School, and Columbia University. From Columbia he received a Doctorate in economics, and was admitted in 1911 to the New York Bar.

In 1910, following several years of newspaper work, Dr. Laidler became Secretary of the Intercollegiate Socialist Society and, eleven years later, Executive Director of the LID, an educational society dedicated to "education for increasing democracy in our economic, political and cultural life." He retired in 1957.

While directing the LID, Dr. Laidler lectured extensively in the nation's colleges; taught economics and labor problems in New York colleges; wrote and edited forty books and pamphlets on social and economic questions—including some college texts; ran for Governor and other offices on the Socialist ticket in New York, and was elected a member of the New York City Council. Closely associated with John Dewey in the LID, the People's Lobby and the League for Independent Political Action, during Dr. Dewey's chairmanship of those organizations, Dr. Laidler served also as chairman of the never-to-be-forgotten Dewey 90th Birthday Dinner. He continues as member of the Board of

Biographical Notes

the National Bureau of Economic Research and the National Housing Conference.

CORLISS LAMONT, writer, teacher, and humanist philosopher, was born in Englewood, New Jersey, in 1902. He was graduated from Harvard in 1924, studied at Oxford for a year, and took his Ph.D. at Columbia in 1932. He is a member of the American Philosophical Association, the American Humanist Association, the Academy of Political Science, the NAACP, and the Clan Lamont Society of Scotland.

A fighter for the traditional freedoms in the American Bill of Rights, Dr. Lamont served for 20 years as a Director of the American Civil Liberties Union. He is now Chairman of the Bill of Rights Fund which he founded, and Vice Chairman of the Emergency Civil Liberties Committee.

His published works include *The Philosophy of Humanism, The Illusion of Immortality, The Independent Mind, Freedom Is as Freedom Does* and other books. He also edited an anthology of poetry, *Man Answers Death*. He has taught at Cornell, Harvard, and the New School for Social Research, and is now a lecturer in philosophy at Columbia University.

ERNEST NAGEL, born in Novemesto, Czechoslovakia, November 1901, was educated in New York City's public schools, The College of the City of New York, and at Columbia University, where he received his M.A. in 1925, and his Ph.D. in 1930. After teaching in the New York City schools from 1923 to 1929, he served a year as instructor in philosophy at The College of the City of New York, and since 1931 has taught at Columbia University where he has been John Dewey Professor of Philosophy since 1954.

A Guggenheim Fellow in 1934–35 and 1951–52, he is now a Fellow at the Center for Advanced Study in the Behavioral Sciences (1959–60). He is also a Fellow of the American Academy of Arts and Sciences, and was President of the Association for Symbolic Logic (1946–48) and of the American Philosophical Association, Eastern Division, 1954. His published works include *On the Logic of Measurement, Introduction to Logic and Scientific*

Method (with Morris R. Cohen), *Principles of the Theory of Probability, Sovereign Reason, Logic Without Metaphysics,* and *Gödel's Proof* (with J. R. Newman).

JOHN HERMAN RANDALL, JR. has taught philosophy at Columbia University since 1920; since 1950 he has served as F. J. E. Woodbridge Professor of Philosophy. He is author of *The Making of the Modern Mind, Nature and Historical Experience, The Role of Knowledge in Western Religion,* and other books, and has written many articles and contributions to co-operative volumes. He has served as Chairman of the Editorial Committee of *The Journal of the History of Ideas,* and as President of the American Philosophical Association, Eastern Division, and of the Renaissance Society of America. He is joint editor of *The Journal of Philosophy*.

Mr. Randall, who first studied with Dewey in 1917, was closely associated with him thereafter as a student, as colleague and friend. On the many occasions he has been called upon to interpret Dewey's thought, he has been able to draw on his familiarity with Dewey's informal views and intellectual personality to throw light on his printed works. Above all, Dewey's writings have come to him against the background of the man, the humble and homespun but shrewd and acute Yankee saint.

HERBERT W. SCHNEIDER was born in Berea, Ohio, on March 16, 1892. He attended The College of the City of New York for one year, then studied at Columbia University, where he took his A.B. in 1915 and his Ph.D. in 1917. Also the holder of an L.H.D. from Union College (1947), Dr. Schneider has taught philosophy and religion at Columbia since 1918, and since 1956 has been a Columbia Professor Emeritus of Philosophy. In 1958–59 a Whitney Visiting Professor at Colorado College, he is now teaching at Pomona College.

During the course of his career Dr. Schneider has been a Rockefeller Research Fellow in Italy (1926–27); a Fulbright Fellow in France (1950); and served in Paris in 1953–56 as head of UNESCO's division of philosophy and humanistic studies. He is a member of the American Philosophical Association and the Church History Society, and a Fellow of the American Academy of Arts and Sciences.

Dr. Schneider co-edits the *Journal of Philosophy*, and among his books are *A History of American Philosophy, Religion in Twentieth Century America, Three Dimensions of Public Morality, The Puritan Mind, Making the Fascist State*, and *A Bibliography of John Dewey* (co-author).

HAROLD TAYLOR, born and raised in Toronto, Canada, attended Toronto public schools and the University of Toronto where he took a B.A. and an M.A. for honors work in philosophy and literature. From 1936 to 1939 Dr. Taylor lived in London where he attended the University of London, taking a doctor of philosophy degree in 1938. In 1939 Dr. Taylor joined the philosophy faculty at the University of Wisconsin, teaching social philosophy and aesthetics for six years, with time out for war service on a research project in psychology.

In 1945, at the age of 30, he became president of Sarah Lawrence College, Bronxville, New York.

Biographical Notes

The College is one of the leading experimental colleges in the United States and Dr. Taylor, like the College he has represented for the past 14 years, is known for the vigor and originality of his educational ideas along with the progressive quality of his thinking in politics and social philosophy. Following his retirement from the Sarah Lawrence presidency this year, Dr. Taylor will resume his teaching and writing in the field of philosophy and education.

MILTON HALSEY THOMAS is University Archivist of Princeton University. He was born in Troy, and holds Columbia University degrees in arts, library science, and U.S. history. For three years he was librarian of the Butler Library of Philosophy at Columbia, during which time he compiled *A Bibliography of John Dewey* (1929) with the collaboration of Herbert Wallace Schneider and Dr. Dewey himself. A second edition appeared in 1939, and a third edition is now in preparation.

For over thirty years Mr. Thomas was Curator of Columbiana, the archives of Columbia University, where he assembled a large collection of obscure and fugitive Dewey material. His own writings have been chiefly in the field of American history and biography, and include "The Gibbs Affair at Columbia in 1854," a study in the history of academic freedom; a dozen articles in the *Dictionary of American Biography*, and several compilations of Columbia bibliography and alumni records. He was joint editor, with Allan Nevins, of *The Diary of George Templeton Strong, 1835–1875*, published in four volumes in 1952. His latest work, *The Diary of Samuel Sewall, 1674–1729*, newly edited from the original manuscript in the Massachusetts Historical Society, is now going through the press.